REINVENTING LOCAL NEWS

CONNECTING COMMUNITIES THROUGH
NEW TECHNOLOGIES

by Adam Clayton Powell III
Senior Fellow, Annenberg School for Communication
and
Director, Integrated Media Systems Center
Viterbi School of Engineering
University of Southern California

USC

ANNENBERG

SCHOOL FOR

COMMUNICATION

REINVENTING LOCAL NEWS
CONNECTING COMMUNITIES THROUGH NEW TECHNOLOGIES
By Adam Clayton Powell III
Published by
FIGUEROA PRESS
Suite 401E
840 Childs Way
Los Angeles, CA 90089
Phone: (213) 740-3570
Fax: (213) 740-5203
www.figueroapress.com

Figueroa Press is a division of the USC University Bookstore
Copyright © 2005, all rights reserved
Cover, text and layout design by Jeff Ratto, USC GraphicDesign
Produced by Crestec Los Angeles Inc.
Printed in the United States of America

Library of Congress Cataloguing-in-Publication Data
Powell, Adam Clayton III
Reinventing Local News: Connecting Communities Through New Technologies
Includes appendices
ISBN: 1-932800-15-8

Library of Congress Number: 2005933557

TABLE OF CONTENTS

REINVENTING LOCAL NEWS

USC
ANNENBERG
SCHOOL FOR
COMMUNICATION

PART I: EXECUTIVE SUMMARY

Are you an avid consumer of local news?
Yeah, Because, you know, we've all got to see the storm report.
　　　—Michael Powell, Chairman, Federal
　　　Communications Commission [1.1]

The FCC chairman is a typical viewer: By a large margin, weather holds the most interest for local news viewers and listeners. More than 60 percent of both men and women named the weather as the subject in which they were "very interested," far more than any other subject area, according to a survey [1.2] for the Radio-Television News Directors Association.

But news must be more than weather: The second most important subject, again by a wide margin, was *local* news. More than national news, politics, sports, entertainment or traffic, Americans want local news.

But how well do local broadcasters and Web sites address this need?

How well do they address the fundamental local issues that enable an informed citizenry to make choices on election day?

That is the subject of this report: local news on television, radio and the Internet.

This is not intended to be as comprehensive as, for example, the research reports of the Project for Excellence in

Journalism [1.3]. Based on a year of interviews and research in 2002 and 2003, here are some of the findings:

The best local news on television may not be broadcast. The all-news 24-hour local cable news channels were a more serious, detailed, editorially solid alternative to the traditional 6 and 11 p.m. news broadcasts. Just as all-news radio all but eliminated serious local news on commercial radio (National Public Radio member stations being notable exceptions), all-news local television may begin to eclipse traditional "appointment" local newscasts in years to come.

The best local news on television might not even be on television. The fastest and most complete "television news" in San Diego may well have been the video at SignOnSanDiego. com, the Web site of the San Diego *Union Tribune,* which had its own camera crews, live Webcams and even live helicopter video, all without a television or radio partner. Its video coverage of the 2003 San Diego fires was fast, thorough and continuous. That site also had the second highest audience penetration of any newspaper site in the country, exceeded only by Washingtonpost. com.

The best local news on radio was on all-news and news-talk stations. Whether AM or FM, commercial or non-commercial, the all-news and news-talk stations were the only radio newsrooms with the resources to cover their communities.

The best local news on the Internet was on the Web sites of local daily newspapers. As with radio, it was because those newspapers typically had far more resources devoted to covering their communities than non-newspaper Web sites.

The best local news in all media was associated with the growth of "micro-local news." Instead of being vague and regional, "micro-local" news coverage enabled editors and reporters to identify and cover local issues in a way that personalized broad topics and promoted understanding of their different communities across broad coverage areas. Experiments by the BBC on television and NPR member stations on radio were notable examples.

Underestimating younger audiences. Conventional wisdom among media managers holds that men and women under 50, or even 65, are not interested in local news. As is so often the case, conventional wisdom is wrong. However, media executives may cling to this belief because local news is concentrated on such media as AM radio, newspapers and broadcast television, none of which is favored by younger Americans. Those who use younger-skewing media, such as the Internet or FM radio, found they attracted younger audiences for local news. See especially the experience of Bonneville, detailed in section 3.5, below.

Local news is now global. Micro-local news could draw an audience that exceeded editors' expectations, both in number and in geographic reach. Whether "country of origin" news for recent immigrants or micro-local news for a global audience, the old truism "telling the big story by telling the small story" achieved a new resonance.

Local news needs innovation. Over and over, news executives interviewed for this report noted a lack of innovation and experimentation in local news. Many cited the experience of WBBM-TV in Chicago, which introduced a very different format for its nightly 10 p.m. news in 2000, dropping crime and tabloid stories [1.4]. The audience rejected WBBM-TV's new format —also, some critics called it dull—and WBBM-TV returned to a more conventional local news format in 2001. [1.5]

However, of that minority who are trying to reinvent local news—some are profiled in this report—many found journalistic success, increased audiences and higher revenue. Not all experiments succeeded, of course, but lack of experimentation often led to eroding audiences and revenue.

"Every other genre [on TV] is constantly reinventing itself," said Nigel Kay [1.6], who runs BBC regional news, with the exception of local television news, which he described as essentially the same as in the 1970s and overdue for reinvention. "If we [journalists] don't do it, there is no reason someone else won't do it."

One large caveat: This report is a snapshot from a twelve-month period starting in mid-January 2003, focusing primarily on the U.S. No one really knows the future, so predictions by the most august or humble must be taken with a very large grain of salt. However, this can be a source of joy, as the fictional mathematician Valentine exclaimed with pleasure in Tom Stoppard's play *Arcadia:* "It's the best possible time to be alive, when almost everything you thought you knew is wrong." [1.7]

PART II: LOCAL TELEVISION NEWS –
EXCERPTS OF A POSSIBLE FUTURE

At 3 p.m. on 2 November 1936 the BBC inaugurated the first television service in the world. There were speeches, jugglers, and comedy dancers. At 9 p.m. Leslie Mitchell introduced the first edition of "Picture Page," "a magazine of general and topical interest." Thus at the very beginning of television non-fiction was prominent, but already nudging up against more obviously entertainment-oriented programming.

—*Television: An International History* [2.1]

2.1 Introduction

Many television viewers and broadcast journalists no longer worry about local news "nudging up against" entertainment, as was the case in 1936. Instead, they are concerned that entertainment-oriented programming has become an integral part of local news on television. And there is the widespread worry that the rise of show business considerations contribute to the worsening quality of local television news, according to Pew research in 2002:

"In a survey of 103 news directors nationwide, fully half said they felt their profession was heading down the wrong track, while only a third felt that it was on the right track." [2.2]

Today there are numerous opportunities to reverse this trend and to improve local news on television, including emulating best practices at leading stations and cable operators around the U.S. and in other countries; reaching out to connect with viewers and community institutions; and exploiting new computer-based technologies and a broadly distributed video and data infrastructure that reach into most viewers' homes.

Certainly local television journalists have reason to worry: The audience is fragmenting as more channels and video choices appear, and the audience for local television news is aging—not as rapidly as the network audience, but aging nonetheless. Meanwhile, 24-hour local news channels in two dozen U.S. cities are gaining audiences and revenues, somewhat at the expense of the broadcasters who offer "appointment" local news. As these local news channels proliferate, some are predicting the marginal or lowest-audience local news broadcasts will become economically unsustainable.

This would repeat the pattern of all-news stations' growth in commercial and then public radio over the past four decades, growth that all but eliminated traditional "appointment" local news on the vast majority of radio stations in cities across the U.S.

Television executives need only look over their shoulders at newspaper data to see what could happen to them. There is an even more dramatic shift in the news audience in print: the loss of the under-40 audience by daily newspapers. Only 30% of Americans in their 30s now read a daily paper, down from 53% ten years ago. And ten years ago, the penetration rate for those in their 20s—today's thirtysomethings—was 48%, so more than a third of them actually *stopped reading* newspapers, according to the Pew Research Center's biennial news survey in 2002 [2.3].

"The audience, the delivery and the economics are all changing," said Deborah Potter, executive director of NewsLab [2.4] and co-author of the Pew report, and those changes are all exerting powerful forces that are reshaping—some say squeezing—local television news. Stations have reacted by reducing resources assigned to local news. And one of the largest broadcast groups, Sinclair, was experimenting on its television stations in 2003 with "Centralcasting," "local" newscasts produced entirely at Sinclair's news headquarters in Maryland. [2.5] The "Centralcasting" experiment may or may not prove financially successful. Many journalists believe (and many hope) it will not be a successful local news service. [2.6]

But local television news faces pressure from a related and growing problem: As the financial barriers to entry drop, with the cost of video production and distribution plunging, incumbent local news providers must innovate to retain and expand their audience and their business. In addition to new local cable news channels, we now see additional new providers of local video news, such as radio stations, newspapers and even government agencies and community groups.

2.2 Practices, Tools and Innovations to Re-Empower Journalists

1. BEST PRACTICES. The Local Television News Project in 2002 published the most complete content analysis of local newscasts, noting a correlation between quality journalism and larger audiences: "A five-year study of local television that analyzed more than 1,200 hours of news and more than 30,000 stories suggests that by several measures, quality, as defined by broadcast journalism professionals, is the most likely path to commercial success, even in today's difficult economic environment." [2.7]

So one place to start with best practices was to look at some examples, in that analysis and elsewhere:

—In New York City, news directors Paula Madison [2.8] and Will Wright [2.9] were cited for their work in the 1990s attracting the largest audiences for WNBC and WWOR, respectively, in their time periods—5, 6 and 11 p.m. for WNBC,

10 p.m. for WWOR. Madison and Wright achieved ratings and revenue success by airing the most solid broadcast journalism in the city, augmented by award-winning investigative journalism.
    —In the San Francisco Bay Area, KTVU's top-rated 10 p.m. newscast actually *gained* viewers when news director Andrew Finlayson and political editor Randy Shandobil added long-form, in-depth reporting on candidates and issues in the 2002 election.   KTVU also was cited in an analysis [2.10] showing superior political journalism can attract audiences. The station also provided its political coverage, for free, to every station in California via a satellite feed that any station in the state could use, reaping additional prestige if not immediate revenue.   (Note: Among the awards KTVU won for its coverage was the Walter Cronkite Award for Excellence in Television Political Journalism, awarded by the USC Annenberg School [2.11].)
    —Among the major broadcast groups, those interviewed consistently gave Belo, Hearst and Scripps stations the highest marks for good journalism in their respective cities, and those groups' stations are also audience and financial leaders in their markets. An analysis by the Project for Excellence in Journalism [2.12] suggested larger group owners are not providing their viewers with superior journalism. But some station groups— again Belo was mentioned frequently—leverage their multiple local newsrooms to provide more in-depth stories for viewers.
    —Local 24-hour news channels are now available to viewers in more than two dozen regions [2.13], from New York 1 [2.14] and the Cablevision News Channel 12 services in Connecticut, New Jersey and Long Island [2.15], serving the most populous local area in the U.S., to news channels in cities as small as Albany, NY, according to an annual survey [2.16] by the National Cable and Telecommunications Association. Those who work at the 24-hour local channels and those in broadcast newsrooms who compete with them point to the local news

channels as sources of solid coverage of breaking news, beat reporting and enterprise features.

"They're the only local news worth watching," said Stephen C. Miller, assistant to the technology editor at *The New York Times* and a former television news manager at CBS News and Channel 9 in Washington [2.17]. One reason: geographically focused coverage.

"The problem is that stations have a mandate to cover areas that are too big," said Paul Sagan [2.18], who stepped down as news director of WCBS-TV in New York City to start New York 1 in 1992. "The trend at regional news channels is to cover one city, one government."

These channels also exhibited a different relationship to the audience: For example, Robin Smythe [2.19], general manager of Orlando's 24-hour news channel, said her newsroom served "customers," not "viewers."

—Low-power television broadcasters, operating well under the radar of most media watchers, are providing narrowcast news and information to demographically targeted audiences, typically recent immigrants, providing both local news service and "country of origin" news via satellite—or on tape shipped by air from Central America to Los Angeles. KSFV, a low-power station on channel 26 in Los Angeles, serves immigrants from El Salvador and Guatemala. According to Paul Koplin [2.20], president and CEO of Venture Technologies Group LLC, which owns channel 26, the service includes daily newscasts from Central America, live call-in programs with the consuls general, special coverage of local health fairs and a live broadcast of the annual Los Angeles Central American Day Parade, which Koplin said attracts 500,000 people.

Spanish-language newscasts are available in major cities on stations affiliated with the Univision and Telemundo networks. Despite attracting large audiences—sometimes the largest local television news audience at 6 or 11 p.m. in cities including New York [2.21]—these have not been the focus of attention by most traditional journalism analysts. And all but ignored by mainstream media are local television newscasts in such languages as Korean, Japanese and Chinese, available over the air in a few cities, such as San Francisco, and on cable in much of the United States. [2.22]

Public television stations as a group were less active in local news than their public radio counterparts—and far less than the national PBS network, which provides daily world and national news coverage. So while television stations affiliated with the major commercial networks produced two, three or more hours of local news per day, with a few exceptions—WGBH-TV in Boston was one—public television stations did not offer daily coverage of local and regional news.

More detailed accounts of best practices in local television have been compiled by Tom Rosenstiel and Bill Kovach at the Project for Excellence in Journalism [2.23] and by Dave Iverson [2.24], among others. "Best Practices for Television Journalists" [2.25] by Av Westin is now out of print and hard to find, but it is worth the effort to locate a copy. And many stations have booklets or brochures, such as WGBH's "Guide to Bias-Free Communications," [2.26] which can be useful.

Partnerships across media have proven valuable for the broadcasters, cable operators and newspapers that have joined to form them. In Chicago, New England and Florida, noted Greg Klein [2.27], who directs research for the National Cable Television Association, joint newsrooms provide reporting for a daily newspaper, a local television station, the local 24-hour news channel and sometimes a local radio station as well, combining resources to provide far deeper coverage than a television newsroom alone could provide.

Klein and Sagan noted the failure of the 24-hour local news channel serving Orange County [2.28] could be traced at least in part to its unique lack of partners. The channel was started by a newspaper, the *Register*, with neither a cable nor a broadcast news partner; in the end, the stand-alone channel could not survive financially. (And early in 2003, the parent company that owns the *Register* was put up for sale.)

Another 24-hour local news channel went dark in California, and it failed for similar reasons. Bay TV [2.29], the local public affairs channel serving the San Francisco Bay Area, had been operated by KRON-TV, then the NBC affiliate, and KRON's co-owned daily newspaper, the *San Francisco Chronicle*. But after the Chronicle company sold KRON to Young Broadcasting, the new owners lost the NBC affiliation and KRON became a money-losing station, according to industry financial analysts. Soon after taking over KRON, without a newspaper partner, the new owners pulled the plug on Bay TV.

But Bay TV and Orange County were among the few exceptions, and they emphasized the crucial role of cross-media partnerships.

Another form of local news partnership emerged in experiments where public television stations began cooperating with commercial and public radio stations. For example, the Gannett-owned stations in Washington, D.C., and Phoenix formed partnerships with local public television stations in their areas to provide more political and election news together than they otherwise would have provided separately. And NBC's local newsroom in Washington furnished live election night reports in the fall of 2002 to Howard University's public television station, WHUT-TV. [2.30]

Klein noted 24-hour long-form information channels, some modeled after C-SPAN, have been started with partners including municipalities and government agencies [2.31]. He also pointed to university-run channels, such as George Mason University's GMU-TV in Virginia, which provide community information along with classroom and other educational programming. But with some exceptions—again, GMU-TV is an example, and the Illinois Channel is another—these channels were not launched to provide a local news service.

Another form of partnership is starting to multiply, across different television outlets serving demographically different audiences: Co-owned NBC and Telemundo are now sharing resources, as are CBS News, MTV and Black Entertainment Television, also co-owned. Similar partnerships could be formed with such similarly demographically focused services as TV One, an African-American-oriented cable network that began in January 2004 [2.32], BlackPressUSA, the national reporting hub of African-American-owned newspapers [2.33], and MBC Cable Network's [2.34] black-oriented MBC News Channel [2.35] could attract similar partnerships.

2. RECONNECTING WITH THE ISSUES. At newsroom after newsroom, those cited for best practices were those ascertaining and focusing on the important issues and concerns of their communities. Those were also the newsrooms that did not focus on crime and police blotter stories, which have become a staple in many local TV newsrooms, according to data compiled by the Local Television News Project [2.36].

"The opportunities are to get back to coverage of important issues and get away from crime coverage," said Marty Haag [2.37], who retired in 2000 [2.38]. Until his death in 2005, he preached as a teacher what he had practiced as a longtime Belo news manager who brought both ratings and awards to his stations.

"What I would hope would happen." said Haag, "is that television stations would get back to beat reporting and not expect everybody to be a general assignment reporter. ...We don't have people working regular beats and getting to know the principals in a discipline. I would hope those stations in markets 25 and above—maybe it should be markets 30 or 40 and above—if there are not beats that are covered every day, there are areas of interest that a reporter should know ... and work that the way traditionally a newspaper reporter would do it."

Haag said issues-oriented coverage could help stem viewer dissatisfaction with local news.

"I know that horse has been beaten to death," he said, "but it seems all the statistics I have ever seen show there is such a dominance of crime that it has been a major factor in the fact that viewers have turned away from local television news."

Haag said covering issues requires a commitment from the news director as well as the general manager—and a willingness to ignore the advice of many television news consultants.

"There are many, many beats that regularly go uncovered," said Haag. "We have decided over the last ten or fifteen years, based on what data we have gotten back from research from consultants, that there are some beats that are automatically covered in newscasts because they are high-profile, such as medicine, health and consumer. But there are all sorts of beats, like growth and what happens as a city expands," that are not covered.

Haag pointed to the Project for Excellence data that showed more than a quarter of all local news is devoted to reports on crime, the highest percentage in years, while stations devote less than 1% of their stories to such issues as aging and Social Security, welfare or the arts. [2.39] And he singled out one issue that, also at less than 1%, he said is especially overlooked:

"The issue of race is probably one of the most difficult facing the United States, and has been since God knows when, and we kind of dance around it," he said. "Local stations say that is not a 'television story,' or let the networks cover that." According to the Project for Excellence data [2.39], fewer than 0.5% of local news stories concerned race.

Haag was among many citing the importance of original enterprise and investigative reporting, pointing to his Belo experience as evidence stations may not need to make a huge investment to make a large impact.

"I'm particularly proud of what KHOU-TV [Belo's Houston television station] did," he said. "It's just two or three people. They not only broke the [Ford] Explorer story, they have gotten people out of prison because of faulty lab work by Houston police. I just hope we get serious again."

And answering critics who have said investigations on television always require large budgets, Haag said some of the best work can be found in small towns, where local news budgets are necessarily limited.

"You don't have to have a hundred people on staff to do these things," he said. "The first thing is to have people who are visionaries. How do these stations do this and get away with this—and make it work—when there are so many others just plodding along doing the same thing?"

Some point to inexperienced news managers at many major-market local newsrooms.

"The major problem with television news is that television news management has not paid its dues," said Stephen Miller. "For all of the criticism of newspapers, most of the news management worked their way to the top. You have no 28-year-old executive editors. If you have some kid who produced a great newscast in Peoria and a year later he's producing or news director in Cleveland, he's never been out on a story, and he hasn't been in town long enough to know the nuances."

And Haag pointed to a lack of vision.

"Eugene Roberts [2.40] once said a good newspaper knows something about itself," said Haag. "I think that ought to be the motto of a good news director. He ought to be in a position to tell viewers what is really going on in the city, what is happening that will directly affect you, your pocketbook, on the political front. It's more than just the one-dimensional murder du jour."

3. RECONNECTING WITH THE COMMUNITY. Local television is uniquely powerful in its ability to convene and connect, and local news can benefit from exploiting this potential. Some effective tools are simple and well known: Ombudsmen, community advisory committees and community breakfast and lunch meetings all have long histories.

"There's no substitute for face time" is the advice from a PBS Web site [2.41] that included best practices at local newsrooms. On the same site, local reporters were urged to get out of the office and the anchor studio to visit "barbershops, schools, churches and community centers."

This is not a new concept. For decades, Westinghouse Broadcasting (which later acquired CBS and then merged with Viacom) required every news director, public affairs director and station manager at each of its stations to have a minimum number of face-to-face interviews every year with elected and appointed community officials to discuss community issues. This was far in excess of "ascertainment" requirements then mandated by FCC regulations. At a very basic level, it familiarized managers with issues and the players in their communities. And in city after city, Westinghouse stations outperformed their competitors in local news audiences, awards and revenue.

"What works best in local news is knowing the people —both the players and the citizens," said Kojo Nnamdi [2.42], who has been a local news anchor on Washington, D.C., public television and radio stations for more than three decades. "By which I mean, all too often, local leaders are characterized more by their official positions than by who they are. If the news agency editor or reporter knows the people, they can be three-dimensional, they can be real. And people are interested in real people."

"The second thing," Nnamdi continued, "is knowing places and what places mean to people. When people read about real places, that means something. Whenever you have issues presented that way, it means something to them."

This is where many point to the local 24-hour news channels, saying knowledge of their neighborhoods is one of the special strengths of local all-news television. [2.43]

"If you start covering your neighborhood, you're going to do a better job than if you just show up in the newsroom," said Stephen Miller of *The New York Times*, a Brooklyn resident. "If you live in Brooklyn or you live in Queens, and you have some idea that Ridgewood is right on the border, you know there's a really interesting dynamic about that neighborhood."

Telling the big stories through the lens of a community is also a time-honored tool for journalists, and reconnecting with the community can enhance this form of storytelling.

"You can really tell how major trends and what is happening in aging or poverty… can be personified and localized and show in a very effective way how this impacts individuals and really plumb deeply into the major issues," said Haag.

Even such broad national questions as free speech and the Constitution can easily be translated into strong local and micro-local news, according to Paul K. McMasters, First Amendment Ombudsman at the Freedom Forum and former president of the Society of Professional Journalists. [2.44]

"Every day there is at least one emotionally compelling and highly reportable First Amendment story in every community," said McMasters. "Banning books in the school library, public libraries and the Internet, posting the Ten Commandments in public buildings: These stories are myriad in number and highly diverse in content, the very kind of story that transfixes but also helps bring about community solutions. They would give a highly telegenic option to crime and gore. One of the beats could be the library. Another could be the local religious network. Another would be parents' organizations."

Broadening the traditional definition of newsmaker can also be fruitful. Local news is made not just by elected officials but what Richard C. Harwood [2.45] called "Connectors," "Catalysts" and "Experts," such as doctors, lawyers and teachers. [2.46]

"Local news is also about local information, and I really think people are less interested in traditional news," said Jan Schaffer [2.47], executive director of the Institute for Interactive Journalism at the University of Maryland [2.48] and longtime director of the Pew Center for Civic Journalism [2.49]. "They are looking for information that has far more utilitarian value. And they are looking for ways to make choices that make a difference in the community."

Connecting to "soft" community institutions such as libraries, parks, museums and cultural centers can provide stories, leads and local information that viewers prize. Recent research for public radio [2.50] found audiences wanted stories reflecting the connectedness of their communities—how people and institutions connect to each other. And they were often highly critical of "local news and local talk shows" that seemed disconnected.

From the sports and business desks comes somewhat similar advice: Drop routine coverage that viewers get elsewhere or package it separately. That means playing down that nightly Dow Jones average—anyone who really cares already knows it, and in more detail—and could even apply to sports, which is of interest to a small percentage of the audience.

"I'm convinced that the newspaper that starts to set itself apart in the 21st century is going to be the first newspaper that has the *cojones* to drop [daily] game stories and to go with analysis," said John Marvel, vice president and executive editor, ESPN.com [2.51].

Applying his advice to local television, that means nightly newscasts should focus on business and sports stories and investigative reports that would make page one of the local newspaper, leaving the daily stock prices and basketball scores to the Internet—and, of course, to sports channels such as ESPN.

In Europe, a variation on this trend is finding acceptance: The BBC began experimenting in 2002 with a "more intimate style of reporting" in its local television newscasts, according to Nigel Kay [1.6], redirecting BBC journalists to give a "much higher precedence to individuals" rather than such institutional staples as the police news conference or the mayor's statement, to provide stories describing the impact of institutions on citizens.

"What's in it for me?" Kay asked, looking at a story of a 17-year-old who died of a drug overdose. "How can I make the story relate to every parent? We have to give them useful advice." But, he added, he wanted to accomplish this without turning BBC local newscasts into a series of "victim journalism" reports.

Kay said local television news has lost 4.5 million viewers from 1999 to 2002 in the U.K., most of the loss coming from the BBC's principal competitor, the commercial ITV network. Most of the lost viewers, according to Kay, were in homes with multichannel cable and satellite. While the BBC was still leading commercial competitor ITV in 13 of the U.K.'s 14 local regions—Northern Ireland was the one exception—Kay said it was time for change.

The innovations in BBC local news (see "Connecting at the Neighborhood Level," 2.6, below), were part of an effort to look three to five years into the future and experiment with new techniques that might be fully implemented by the middle of the decade. But BBC news managers said audiences increased sharply in the test areas where this technique was introduced, so the network was planning to expand "personal" storytelling throughout the U.K. in 2004, in an effort to differentiate its news service from anything else on British television.

4. RECONNECT WITH YOUNGER AUDIENCES. "Nobody" is attracting young news viewers, according to Deborah Potter. "There's a real open question: Ten years from now, who's doing news for them?"

One answer is to cover stories that are made by and hold a strong interest for young people. Nancy Maynard, former co-owner of the *Oakland Tribune,* wrote about this problem confronted by newspapers [2.52], and Stephen C. Miller, who went from local and network television newsrooms to cover technology for *The New York Times*, urged local stations to cover the culture of young Americans before the audience erodes further.

"If you look and watch the kids who are hanging out, dressing alike, listening to the same music, it cuts across class, race, economics and gender," Miller said. "This is the first time I've seen the kids not just listening to the same music but hanging out together. We're going to have a whole generation with adopted cultural norms from ethnic groups that 20 years ago wouldn't have been caught dead together."

MTV discovered it began to attract young viewers to MTV News by covering their peers and focusing on stories of interest to them, such as the environment and South Africa (remember, this was the early 1990s). It also didn't hurt that MTV's anchors were not 70 years old. Dan Rather and Tom Brokaw were well past the retirement age in other professions, and Peter Jennings first anchored ABC's evening network newscast four decades ago, before most of ABC Television's target audience was born.

At the local level, WAMU radio in Washington was among broadcasters experimenting with MTV's approach to covering young people, starting a local news service called "Teen Voices."

"Teen Bureaus [groups of young journalists] will tell their stories," said Susan Clampitt, former general manager and executive director, WAMU Radio [2.53]. She said the new reports would be good for radio and good for the community.

"There are enough studies out showing that using a tabloid style is good for a quick [ratings] hit, then you're back in third place trying to scratch your way back up," said Miller. "I want to reach those kids who say they never watch television, but they do watch television. They say they don't read newspapers, but they do read newspapers—online."

5. CONNECTING AT THE NEIGHBORHOOD LEVEL. Television stations in larger cities cover such a large geographical area that they are no longer truly local. (See "local 24-hour news channels" in 2.2, above.)

"It's so hard to do stories that people can react to," said Paul Sagan, who noted New York, Chicago and Philadelphia are among cities where viewers might not have any tie to the governments being covered in their local news. Sagan said he could imagine viewers exclaiming, "'It's not even my state!'"

"One of the roles the hyper-local cable channels can fill is they can do stories that are relevant," he added, noting each local news channel can focus on a particular local government.

"Some cities are next to impossible to cover," said Marty Haag, "because they are so large, so diverse, that news organizations have never wrestled with how to create a threshold of relevance for stories in one particular area and bring that to [the] interest level of people in the general audience...."

Miller has managed television newsrooms in New York and Washington and is familiar with multi-jurisdiction regions, with added complexities trying to cover local news based in the nation's capital.

"The complication is that [in Washington, D.C.] you are dealing with three states, who knows how many municipalities, plus D.C.," Miller said. "In New York, if you call the police, you call the New York City police department and maybe the transit police. In D.C., I had to call the D.C. cops, the [U.S.] Park Police, the federal cops, the Secret Service. If memory serves, there are 27 various law enforcement agencies. So if you are the local assignment editor trying to make cop calls, that's three hours right there. Crime happens, and you could be dealing with three or four different police jurisdictions. It's a nightmare."

Then there is the issue of relevance.

"In some of these large cities," said Haag, "news directors wrestle with the idea that people in Pasadena don't care what happened in Thousand Oaks, the people in the Bronx don't give a whit for what happened in Yonkers. How can we take a story that comes out of your neighborhood and say to the viewer this is something of trends and of pressures and of concerns of people all over this city? You have to get the news directors to say, 'Short of zoning [see "zoned" newscasts, below], what is the threshold of relevance to get stories that are of interest to the public at large?'"

One way to reach that threshold of relevance is to do the small story that tells the big story. How one neighborhood school or hospital or park copes with budget cuts this year can be relevant to viewers throughout the area, according to Ed Fouhy, executive director and editor of Stateline.org [2.54].

"The state budget crisis is a good story," he said. "It affects everybody. Imagine what will happen when Medicaid benefits are cut."

Fouhy's Web site tracks policy and trends at the state level, and he said abstract spending stories from Springfield or Austin or Sacramento can be made concrete and very understandable when the neighborhood-level effects are covered. He also pointed to the release of census data, which provided a wealth of data on every community in the U.S., data that can be the foundation for stories on how neighborhoods are changing.

Combining a beat system with on-the-ground contacts can produce relevant stories. But looking at the flipside, local newsrooms without that combination can miss stories that affect their viewers every day.

"There are a lot of little things that slip through," said Miller. "The city gets sued over some statute that nobody seems to know about that has a huge impact on tax rates and development. Something gets rezoned and suddenly it's turned into a place where they have gambling and X-rated video parlors. It's stuff like that that needs to be covered."

Bill Kovach, founding director of the Committee of Concerned Journalists [2.55], suggested a new and cost-effective way for local television news to connect with neighborhoods: innovative stringer networks that drill down into the community, starting with political coverage.

"Try to develop a new kind of political reporting," said Kovach. "Each person (journalist) should find ten friends to serve as stringers. Much campaigning now occurs in people's homes, with direct mail and phone calls. It would be a whole new way of developing a network."

Politicians and their consultants have mastered the mass media by circumventing them, according to Kovach.

"Much of the campaign has disappeared from public space and moved into private space," he said, and these local stringer networks would report on that subterranean politics.

"When the New York Times bought the Gannett paper north of Atlanta, we ran them out of town" by reporting community news, said Kovach, who then edited the *Atlanta Journal-Constitution*. Kovach said local television, one way or another, should start covering such community staples as school athletics, school menus, bowling alleys, local street closings and church schedules and sermon topics.

One way to address this issue is to produce "zoned" newscasts or news segments for different communities in a station's coverage area, just as newspapers produce different zoned editions for different neighborhoods. Some of the stories seen in Pasadena or Thousand Oaks would be *about* Pasadena or Thousand Oaks. And some of those stories would be seen *only* in the community "zone" where they originate.

Deborah Potter pointed to another variation: In Lexington, Kentucky, and other smaller cities, local high school sports scores are scrolled in text during the local sports segment of the 10 or 11 p.m. newscasts. And in the future, this text information could be "zoned" or coded to provide neighborhood school scores only to to viewers who live in that particular neighborhood.

Local cable companies already televise micro-local "zoned" advertisements, as well as neighborhood-level public access programs, beamed to specific target communities. They could simply extend "zoned" feeds from advertising to journalism.

Distribution of these "zoned" micro-local newscasts and service segments also could be accomplished via multiplexed broadcasting over the new digital television channels, which support more than one program simultaneously, and by broadband Internet service.

"The cable systems can zone newscasts now, so maybe that is a technological change that will facilitate coverage in these larger cities," said Haag, adding a cautionary note: "It seems to me the staffs would have to be larger, which in this economic climate does not seem a possibility."

But it was the superior local journalism at the 24-hour local news channels that was cited repeatedly by journalists who work for them—and by journalists who compete with them at broadcast stations. Also praised was their predictability, almost news on demand, as opposed to the "appointment viewing" schedule of broadcast station newscasts.

"It's very local," said Potter. "It looks like the old radio news wheel. What's old is new again."

Steve Paulus, senior vice president and general manager of New York 1 [2.56], said he has a staff of 160, larger than any of the competing television stations. In Orlando, there are 100 staff members at the 24-hour local news channel, according to Robin A. Smythe, general manager of Central Florida News, and that number seemed typical even in smaller cities.

These large news channel staffs were deployed as efficiently as possible, using innovative automation to minimize production crews. Paulus recalled a 30-person production crew was required by union contracts and by custom for the one-hour 6 o'clock news broadcast he produced at WCBS-TV. By contrast, he said, New York 1 uses as few as three people in the control room and three others in the newsroom, all producing multiple hours of local news. That difference meant he could hire more street reporters, a total of 28, to cover the city of New York. With a staff that large, Paulus said he could field a beat system more comprehensive than competing television broadcasters—and more elaborate than competing all-news WINS or WCBS radio in New York. New York 1 even had six reporters devoted full-time to covering city politics.

New York 1 announced its beat system explicitly and with evident pride on its Web site:

"Unlike most television stations, NY1 assigns its reporters using the beat system often found at newspapers. NY1 News beats are either geographical or topical: the geographic beats include each of the five boroughs, while the topical beats include health, technology, mass transit, law enforcement, entertainment, neighborhoods, education and business. The political beat is one of NY1's strongest, with five reporters assigned fulltime to the comings and goings at City Hall and one reporter based in the state capital in Albany.

"NY1's reporters all have a connection to New York City. They were born here, lived here or went to school here. They live in the neighborhoods that they cover. They also shoot their own stories, and have become a familiar sight to New Yorkers as they arrive on the scene toting their camera, tripods and batteries.

"In adopting the beat system, NY1 was determined to get away from the 'rip and read' type of journalism often seen on television news. NY1 beat reporters are expected to find their own stories, and are given the time to develop leads. As a result, NY1 is much more than sensational stories or crime news. Some local TV news stations believe in the slogan 'if it bleeds it leads' —but not NY1." [2.57]

In Chicago, the local 24-hour cable news channel is ChicagoLand (CLTV), owned by the Tribune Company, which also owns the *Chicago Tribune* and WGN radio and television. Unlike New York 1, CLTV can draw on resources of co-owned newspaper and television newsrooms. Nevertheless, CLTV posted a statement of editorial policy similar to the statement by New York 1:

"At CLTV, we take the time to do it right! Focused on delivering news and information in a style devoid of any degree of hype or sensationalism, CLTV is truly a reflection of the communities we report in.

"No other station places such special emphasis on the people, places and stories that make ChicagoLand and its surrounding communities so unique." [2.58]

Some of this philosophy can find its way into broadcast television newsrooms. Kim Godwin, former vice president and news director at KNBC-TV in Los Angeles [2.59], said she was trying to get more reporters to "reconnect with the community."

"Local reporters have to get back to basics," she said.

But Sagan, who started the beat system at New York 1, said his model was not at all from broadcast news; he termed his assignment structure "newspaper beats," including governments, education and subways and buses.

Jonathan Knopf, news director and general manager of News 12 New Jersey [2.60], said his channel has an I-team that was given two months to develop each investigative story, then to produce seven-minute stories.

Sagan said he also never hired reporters who were new to New York City, and he required reporters to live where they worked if it was a geographic beat. The New York 1 reporter covering the borough, or county, of Staten Island covered it much better, he said, because the reporter lived there. And those resident reporters can connect with their neighbors. This, in turn, led to a very different style for New York 1.

The station even grouped its local beats on a separate section [2.61] of its Web site, a prelude to a tailored micro-local news service. Tampa's Bay News 9 was another 24-hour local news channel offering a tailored micro-local service. [2.62] Bay News 9 was in the forefront of television newsrooms providing multiple local news channels, according to Barbara Cochran, president of the Radio-Television News Directors Association [2.63]. In addition to its micro-local neighborhood services, Cochran pointed to Tampa's multiple weather channels [2.64] and Spanish-language news service [2.65].

But for now, 24-hour local news channels such as New York 1 are fielding large and cost-effective reporting staffs.

"You're covering news," said Sagan. "You're not doing promos or sweeps or ratings. You're doing it very straight."

"Since it's 24 hours a day," said Miller, "you have to do a lot of reporting, because you have so much time to fill. You can do some of the smaller stories that would be passed over, so you can do the little feature about the bodega on the corner where everyone seems to love the guy and hang out. And that's an interesting story about who he is and who's in the neighborhood."

From the start, New York 1 also relied on heavy repetition of weather, traffic and other features, including its highly promoted "weather on the ones," weather forecasts at :01, :11, :21 and so on, around the clock. [2.66] Borrowed from New York's all-news WINS radio, which has broadcast weather and traffic at ten-minute intervals "on the ones" for decades, New York 1's "clock" has been copied by local news channels around the country.

"Weather on the ones was a slam-dunk for us," said Central Florida News' Robin Smythe, who observed that even sunny central Florida has enough weather news to attract repeat viewers to her station.

In the future, local television news might deliver multiple "zoned" feeds to overlapping geographic areas, based on viewers' interests. Michael Lasky, managing director of the Stargazer Group [2.67], described research he helped coordinate for a micro-local video news service being developed by telephone companies, a service that the phone companies eventually decided not to produce. Although the service never launched, the audience research was of interest, as it showed sharply diverging news interests within each neighborhood.

For example, he said research uncovered a major divide on sports: Many wanted sports results from high schools and even elementary schools in the micro-local zone, but others had no interest in school sports. Instead, for them "sports" meant information, such as whether the local tennis courts or skating rinks were busy—and whether viewers could find a tennis partner or pickup basketball game at the time they wanted. But the more tailored information a service provides, the more costs rise.

Some micro-local newscasts have begun service on a truly neighborhood scale, fueled by tiny budgets and volunteers. Some can be found in such contained communities as retirement homes.

"Our angle is people you know," said Tom Moore, station manager of cable channel 99 serving the Riverview Erickson Retirement Community in Washington, D.C.'s, Maryland suburbs [2.68]. Serving just one thousand potential viewers, channel 99 televises a daily news and information program, which is repeated at least three times each day. The newscasts focus on visitors, lectures and the most popular single feature: the daily cafeteria menus.

Channel 99 also provides a dedicated channel for the community chapel, with a robot camera operated remotely by a joystick, along with 40 or 50 special programs each month.

"The Easter bonnet parade was a winner," said Brent Hoffman, station manager for a similar cable channel at another Erickson Retirement Community nearby. [2.69] Other popular micro-local programs, according to Hoffman, were "Mind Over Memory," a quiz show that has been running for six years, and "Antique Attic," a shameless copy of PBS' "Antique Roadshow" complete with professional appraisers visiting residents' apartments.

"Poking fun could be sensitive," said Moore. "But for them [the residents] to do it is not a problem."

One reason was that all of these programs were produced *by* the residents.

"We're doing it every day with a staff of two and 20–25 [resident] volunteers," said Moore. As for technical polish, said Moore: "It doesn't matter." Besides, more and more retirees come with video experience.

"Their backgrounds are incredibly rich," Hoffman said. "They know a lot about video."

"I have three residents who have digital editors and mini DV cams in their apartments," said Moore. "They cover the community. They have to make it happen."

6. THE BBC EXPERIMENT. Within conventional television newscast services, the micro-local channels face cost pressures. One way of addressing economic pressures is a practice that has become widespread at the local 24-hour news channels, as well as in broadcast newsrooms in smaller cities: single-

person coverage, with one journalist handling the reporting and photography. Replacing a two- or three-person field crew with one journalist has certainly been economically attractive, and Nigel Kay at the BBC pointed out shifting some of his newsrooms to single-person coverage meant they could cover many more stories on a typical day—and different types of stories.

"They get stories and trends the larger BBC News enterprise misses," said Richard Sambrook, director of BBC News [2.70], "using personal and intimate storytelling." Sambrook said each journalist was developing a very separate individual style, often quite different from the BBC's traditional approach. (Approval of this new style from British labor unions was required.)

Nigel Kay said 500 of the 2,000 journalists in his BBC Nations and Regions news department were scheduled for a "three-week boot camp" to learn both the tools of single-person coverage and the techniques of more personal storytelling.

Kay said one immediate advantage is to differentiate BBC local news from its competitors in commercial television: Before boot camp, he said, a typical regional BBC newsroom had six camera crews. Do the arithmetic: To fill a 30-minute local newscast, Kay calculated, each crew must do 1.5 stories per day—so you cannot take chances an assignment will not yield an on-air segment. As a result, BBC crews were covering a steady diet of news conferences by a small core of regular newsmakers, notably the local police chiefs, whose news conferences were routinely covered by both BBC and ITV crews.

"We are working in a very risk-averse environment," said Kay. "We are playing to other people's news agendas." And because ITV typically has one or two fewer crews in regional newsrooms, it is even more risk-averse, he added. "So we are duplicating each other's programs."

After boot camp, Kay said each newsroom also gets a "modest" increase in staff, so a typical local newsroom goes from six camera crews to more than twenty journalists, some still working in teams, but most shooting and reporting as single-person crews. That means many more stories can be assigned and more stories could be developed over two or three days, he said, and it was "doing something about the depth of our coverage."

"It encourages journalists to take much more risks," said Kay. "In essence they have more time. It's like being back in radio, like being back in newspapers." On the one hand, a reporter "could be shooting several stories at a time," gathering material for an enterprise story. But when big news breaks, Kay said the BBC could now field "multiple cameras on one story" for different perspectives.

"The quality of filmmaking and journalism is at the highest standard," Kay said.

But Deborah Potter expressed misgivings about single-person coverage.

"I'm not convinced you get good journalism," she said. "There's no question it can be done. But does it make a *qualitative* difference?"

Paulus, by contrast, argued the calculation was a simple one: Use single-person coverage to field 28 reporters at New York 1, vs. deploying half as many two-person crews. Paulus maintained that additional reporting staff changed the coverage, the programming and even the very nature of the news channel.

Viewers seem willing to accept the work of single-person coverage and to accept much lower production values if the local news and information are relevant to their needs. Nigel Kay said the most popular micro-local television program at the BBC is a local *radio* newscast, televised each morning using a small camera in the corner of the local radio studio. For years, the local BBC radio breakfast newscast was popular, but now for the first time viewers could switch on their TV sets each morning to watch their favorite radio news reader anchoring the news, in what is obviously still a non-telegenic radio studio.

At the national level, Bloomberg News embraced alphanumeric information in the 1980s to add extraordinarily detailed data to television screens. The national all-news cable channels followed suit after the 9/11 terrorist attacks in New York and Washington. Both Potter and Lasky noted viewers were quite willing to accept alphanumeric information, either as crawls over a newscast or even as full-screen graphics, when the graphics described local street closings, news of the local school or other micro-local service information.

NewsChannel 8, the local 24-hour cable news channel serving the Washington, D.C., area [2.71], has a different strategy than most of its local news counterparts around the country. Operating from the same newsroom as co-owned WJLA-TV, NewsChannel 8 alternates newscasts targeting the District of Columbia, Maryland and Virginia, with each "zoned" newscast delivered only to cable viewers in the geographical area covered by that particular newscast. [2.72]

"It goes back to the start of NewsChannel 8, when it only covered Virginia," said longtime anchor Nathan Roberts [2.73]. As cable distribution expanded to D.C. and Maryland, discrete newscasts were added to cover those new viewers. This model was followed by other news channels in other parts of the country: In New England, Hearst's New England Cable News channel inaugurated a "zoned" channel for the city of Worcester and neighboring central Massachusetts. [2.74]

Many view the local 24-hour news channels as licenses to lose money. Anthony Moor, until recently a reporter at KRON-TV in San Francisco and Bay TV, KRON's local cable channel [2.75], described 24-hour channels as "loss leaders, the way [broadcast] TV news used to be." Now new-media editor of the *Democrat and Chronicle* in Rochester, New York, Moor echoed the views of many that, just as broadcasters once did, the cable channels could focus on journalism and audience service rather than ratings.

But Time Warner, Hearst and other operators of the 24-hour local news channels are not producing these channels out of altruism. While some channels are still losing money—Jonathan Knopf said News 12 New Jersey had yet to turn a profit —many are moneymakers. Robin Smythe said the Orlando channel went into positive cash flow after 20 months and was in the black two years ahead of schedule. Steve Paulus said New York 1 has been profitable for years, so much so that it is now the template for nationwide expansion.

"Time Warner is committed to launching news channels in all parts of the country," Paulus said, noting recent and imminent launches in San Antonio, Houston and three cities in New York State—Albany, Rochester and Syracuse.

These "zoned" 24-hour local news channels make business sense, "if you look at the dual revenue stream," according to Paul Sagan. One revenue stream is from commercials, said Sagan, just as broadcast channels receive commercial revenue. However, Paulus, Smythe and others who run micro-local news channels said they do not receive their fair share of advertising sales, both because of the audience ratings services' failure to measure small audiences correctly and because advertising agencies have not realized the true value of either the size of the micro-local news audience or the value of having commercial messages surrounded by community-oriented news and information services. Smythe said her channel reached more viewers than any broadcast station in Orlando—and more people than read the daily *Orlando Sentinel*—but advertisers still were slow to accept the local news channel's claims of the size of its audience.

In addition to commercial revenue, noted Sagan, local news channels also can reap per-household fees charged by cable companies. Just as local cable companies pay a monthly fee to CNN, ESPN, Nickelodeon and other popular national cable networks to carry them locally, micro-local 24-hour channels can generate carriage revenue from local cable operators.

New York 1 reached 2.2 million subscribers by early 2003, according to Paulus, with 170,000 more scheduled to come online in the Hudson Valley north of New York City. The channel also was scheduled to expand to Albany—that is in addition to the separate all-Albany local news channel, Capital News 9, started by Time-Warner in 2003 [2.76]. New York 1 has been available on the Internet for years, at http://www.ny1.com/, along with a video archive that banked more than 15,000 video clips by mid-2003. And Paulus said he would be delighted if New York 1 went national on cable and satellite to offer expatriate New Yorkers news from home. Expanding the channel's reach can add new per-subscriber revenue at minimal cost, he noted.

When a local cable company launches a local news channel, Sagan said, the motivation is often at least in part a desire to avoid paying those per-household fees to someone else. Sagan pointed to Time Warner's New York 1, which covers New York City and is ringed by Cablevision's News 12 channels covering New Jersey, Long Island, Westchester and Connecticut. Time Warner not only charges Cablevision to carry the New York 1 channel—and some Cablevision systems feel it is essential programming—but also could have faced making payments *to* Cablevision if Cablevision had moved its local news channel into New York City.

They are already marketing against each other: As New York 1 and News 12 seek to expand, they are starting to bump into each other. But so far the competition is quite limited, in a few neighborhoods in New York City and a limited number of localities in northern New Jersey.

"We only do this in communities served by Time Warner Cable—fourteen towns—so it is hyper-local," said Paulus. "Then again, [Cablevision's] News 12 has products in Brooklyn and the Bronx that compete with us." [2.77]

Investing to create all-news cable channels was also an effective defense against "overbuilds"—new cable companies that are competing for viewers in some cities, such as RCN, which competes with Time Warner for cable subscribers in New York City [2.78].

"If you have Time-Warner Cable, you will have New York 1. If you have RCN, you will not have New York 1," is how Paulus summarized Time Warner's pitch to wavering subscribers.

Sagan said 24-hour local news channels are "differentiated programming" that can define the entire cable television industry because no one else can provide these services, at least not yet. In particular, according to Sagan, the micro-local news channels represented effective defensive programming against DirecTV and other satellite operators, which did not have channel capacity to distribute local news channels.

Head to head against local broadcast newscasts, the 24-hour local channels have scored striking gains. Paulus said New York 1 had a larger audience in the morning than WCBS-TV, the local CBS station, and it was making inroads at other times of the day.

"We are the wave of the future," he said, predicting some local broadcast channels in New York and elsewhere would drop their local newscasts as they continue to lose viewers and revenue to the all-news channels.

Paulus said breaking news was attracting more and more viewers to his channel, and he provided an example: At 8 o'clock on a Sunday night, during NBC's 1997 commercial-free broadcast of the movie "Schindler's List," a man tried to take over the observation deck of the Empire State Building. Unable to interrupt the network movie, WNBC-TV ran a crawl about the story across the bottom of the screen. According to Paulus, that prompted thousands to switch channels from NBC to New York 1, which grabbed the audience with live coverage.

The ultimate breaking news story for New York 1 was 9/11, when its audience soared. Paulus said many stayed with the news channel, permanently boosting the number of viewers. "Even our sports show is up," said Paulus, adding that was entirely unexpected.

"Events hammer at broadcasters," explained Smythe. "We make money on breaking news. Broadcasters don't." Smythe added broadcasters try to compete by breaking into entertainment programs with live news coverage. But they lose money from commercials that are bumped, and they alienate viewers who want to watch regular programs.

Local news managers said their news channels were just a beginning: Paulus said New York 1's news coverage and programs will be used to launch new micro-local news channels and Internet-delivered news services. The first spin-off, he said, was a channel for taxi cabs, a joint service with Fox News, which is providing national news. But that is just the start.

"We're perfectly positioned to repurpose video," said Paulus, noting the imminent addition of new automated subsidiary channels and Web sites that cost little or nothing to start, making them highly profitable.

Knopf said he was repurposing News 12 coverage to create five new local news channels to serve cable subscribers who have new digital set-top boxes. In addition to the basic News 12 New Jersey channel, the digital service includes an all-weather channel, a channel devoted to nothing but breaking news, a channel for long-form investigative and health features, an on-demand channel serving a looped video tour of New Jersey and an on-demand channel with clips from the News 12 archive.

Once viewers have access to affordable broadband, whether over cable or Internet, local services soon follow, whether provided by local newsrooms or even government agencies. One reason the BBC selected the city of Hull for the location of its micro-news experiment [2.79] was that, unlike most of the rest of the U.K., Hull had a locally operated telephone system [2.80]. The Hull phone system was privatized ten years ago and spun off to Kingston Communications [2.81] with the Hull city council retaining a significant ownership interest. Residents of Hull were offered broadband service, with more than 300 channels of video, to a pilot group of 12,000 subscribers, according to the BBC. Because distances are short, video could be fed over conventional copper telephone wires.

Local schools had a channel on the system, according to Kay, so they started showing everything from school plays—on demand, using viewers' TV remote controls, to play, stop, rewind or fast forward—to live video chats in the evening where teachers tutor students at their homes, typing in questions via e-mail.

There was even a local drama channel, offering a locally written and produced drama that viewers could watch in daily three-minute episodes—or they could wait and string multiple episodes together into longer segments. It worked so well, said Kay, that in the end the BBC presented it as a 90-minute drama on the national BBC network.

7. INTERACTIVITY. Interactive local news could be as straightforward as a severe weather alert or urgent neighborhood bulletin, prepackaged and preset for delivery by television, e-mail, Instant Messenger and even by telephone, just as airlines can notify passengers of flight delays by e-mail or cell phone. But it can be more:

Local broadcasters are using their Web sites for innovative interactive storytelling, ranging from the trivia quiz features that have long been a staple in print to the more elaborate, such as MSNBC's "You Be the Baggage Inspector" feature, which conveyed a sense of the task facing federal inspectors at busy airports.

Even smaller newsrooms with lower budgets are

experimenting with new interactive tools. Jan Schaffer points to Topeka, Kansas; Myrtle Beach, South Carolina; and Spokane, Washington, as areas where local newsrooms have used interactivity.

"My little paper in Everett, Washington, wants to create a gridlock game for Seattle," she said, referring to that city's notorious traffic jams.

New Hampshire Public Radio was one of the first broadcasters to adopt a "Tax Calculator," an online service that lets residents compute changes in their family tax payments based on various policy alternatives [2.82]. A variation on the tax calculator was the "Budget Builder" [2.83], which lets listeners balance competing needs on the state budget. NHPR also started a popular feature, "My New Hampshire" [2.84], to let each listener identify issues he or she wants to follow. The broadcaster will send tailored e-mail messages of stories produced by the station, as well as links to related stories in other media and even tips on upcoming public hearings.

Younger viewers have been attracted by these new story-telling tools, according to editors, and some say that is both good and bad.

"I don't believe young people today are going to read narrative news stories," said Schaffer. "They have a disinclination to get information that way. They find it easier to get information much more interactively."

Combining Web-based interactivity with local news can be difficult, but it can educate viewers. However, editors will need to make certain they are providing journalism in the new-media mix.

"The challenge for the future of news is to test out what are the interactive entry points, and it may mean something other than the inverted pyramid of news stories," said Schaffer. "I don't think anyone has time for that anymore. So what takes the place of that, and how do you make people smarter?"

In this individualized collage, many have noted the very notion of news has been changing.

"Instead of the reporter being the hunter-gatherer and opening the spigot," Schaffer said, "I think that individuals are foraging for their own news, and they are getting it from very different places—push e-mail, e-mail from friends, drive time radio and Jay Leno. Out of all that assemblage you come up with your sense of 'truth' or what is going on in the world. And that is going to be what the news of the future is. It is going to be their definition of news and not our [journalists'] definition."

These educational interactive features, such as New Hampshire Public Radio's "Tax Calculator," sound expensive, and they can be. But through partnerships, local broadcasters can make them affordable. According to Schaffer, some newsrooms tap local universities, community colleges and magnet high schools, where students work on projects together.

"We tried to see if we can build an unprecedented partnership between news organizations and their local universities, in particular grad students who would be software developers," said Schaffer. "For not a lot of money, say $10,000–$15,000, you could get a grad student to build you a game that would qualify as a class project for the student."

This could illustrate budget choices or regional planning issues—a locally tailored version of Sim City, the computer game that teaches players about running a city while they play the game.

But journalists must take care not to let the opportunity for fun and games lead to a backlash from viewers who perceive a bias in the puzzle.

"It's difficult to be objective in questions," said Stephanie Crockett, a news producer at Viacom's Black Entertainment Television network who designs questions for the BET.com Web site. [2.85] (Example: "Which of the five quotes below did Mike Tyson really say?") "If it's not objective the readers will eat me up—and they have my e-mail address."

Stephen Miller, whose beat at *The New York Times* now includes video games, wondered why his former colleagues in local television have not tried to appeal to the millions of fans of interactive games.

"Kids will play computer games for hours and hours and hours, puzzling through intricate games, not just shoot-em-up, but games where you have to really think how you solve the puzzle, how you deal with a clue," said Miller. "Why can't I make television that is as interesting to that audience?"

8. KNOW WHO YOU ARE—AND AREN'T. Local news is not national news. In 2003, when the space shuttle Columbia broke up over Texas, viewers switched to the networks, not to local television. Even online, local news Web sites by and large did not attract readers, who instead went to cnn.com, nasa.gov and to Instant Messenger and chat.

"When the shuttle broke up, my Web site numbers did not budge from normal weekend stats," said Anthony Moor, who runs the Web site of the daily *Democrat and Chronicle* in Rochester, New York. "And why should they?"

But local news can be global: If the major story of the day is from Central America, local television news in Los Angeles should take notice.

"Local, national and international are merging," said Kim Godwin of KNBC-TV. "Local news is international and national news."

Now, even at a local station, Godwin said the key question the 6 p.m. local news tries to answer is, "What is the world talking about today?"

9. KNOW YOUR AUDIENCE. Traditional television ratings are designed to measure mass audiences for advertising sales. As local television news sources multiply with 24-hour local news, low-power channels and micro news reports, additional tools can replace or supplement Nielsen data.

Larger-audience newscasts can measure audiences with Nielsen ratings, but others may require retail-style per-inquiry (PI) measures. Using PI measurements, each individual response—perhaps a telephone call or an online purchase—is logged and credited to the program or commercial that prompted the inquiry. PI has long been a staple of inexpensive radio time: Where low-audience time periods cannot attract high-priced commercials, stations will settle for selling advertising that generates revenue—sometimes very little, sometimes quite substantial—as listeners call to purchase or inquire about an advertiser's product.

Another variation: Producers of the statewide "California Connected" public television series [2.86] pointed to larger turnouts at public hearings that were previewed on their program as proof not only of the broadcast's audience but also that its audience was moved to take action, according to Val Zavala, vice president of news and public affairs at KCET Television. [2.87]

This could point the way to new methods to measure micro-local news audiences: How many parents turn out at the local school board? How many go to the local hospital to get their flu shots? Is public participation increasing at local parks, arts events, public libraries? If and when micro-local media can aggregate these direct measures, they may rival total Nielsen ratings as indices of audience attention.

2.3 Practices, Tools and Innovations to Empower Audiences

1. PARTNER WITH COMMUNITY INSTITUTIONS. Local news can partner with area universities, community colleges and schools for specific projects (see "Interactivity," 2.2.7 above) that also will involve students—and their parents. This can have immediate benefits in stemming the erosion of younger viewers

(see "Reconnecting With Younger Audiences," 2.2.4 above). And it can enhance the credibility of the local news service: The 2004 Edelman credibility survey showed that "doctors or healthcare specialists, academics, average people and representatives of non-governmental organizations" had more credibility than journalists. [2.88]

But some local newsrooms have discovered that regular daily partnerships with educational institutions can be good journalism and good business. In Rome, the leading daily newspaper *La Repubblica* [2.89] has links to 1,000 schools around Italy, according to Jack Driscoll, editor-in-residence at the MIT Media Laboratory's News in the Future Consortium [2.90], who said this is the largest school news network he has seen. On a large scale, this draws thousands of students into the work of the *Repubblica* newsroom, in effect creating a giant stringer network and linking to students' work on the schools' Web sites from the main *Repubblica* site.

2. GLOBAL CONTEXT. The many "country of origin" newscasts now available on cable and low-power television channels are serving audiences with news from countries from China to Guatemala. These newscasts also are becoming an important element of general-audience news services ranging from Univision and Telemundo (news from Mexico) to PBS (live news from the BBC in London and Deutsche Welle in Germany). But this may only begin to suggest the growth of interest in U.S. communities that follow "country of origin" newscasts—national newscasts from other countries, either fed by satellite or flown to L.A. on tape.

USC Professor Sandra Ball-Rokeach conducts an annual census of media in nine different communities in Los Angeles [2.91], and while she found many neighborhood newspapers include news from South America or Asia, she said her research has found an interesting pattern: No newspaper has as a primary target the *geographic* communities—the neighborhoods they serve [2.92]. Instead, publishers are targeting all of Southern California, or more, with neighborhood editions of newspapers that share essentially the same "country of origin" content at the expense of local news coverage.

Ball-Rokeach noted this placed publishers at economic risk, since "country of origin" news is readily available via the Internet. So as Internet use becomes ever wider, the reason for buying these "neighborhood" newspapers will evaporate.

This also had the effect, according to Ball-Rokeach, of making it possible for recent immigrants to maintain dual identities in a way immigrants a century ago could not manage. In 1900, immigrants could follow homecountry news through local ethnic newspapers across the U.S. Now a growing number of immigrants bypass U.S. publications and follow the news from home by watching or reading coverage direct from faraway news organizations.

Combining global context with local news offers an interesting opportunity for local news, enabled financially by technology that now makes affordable routine news from thousands of miles away. CBS News and South Africa's SABC have used e-mail audio and video attachments since 1999 to bypass satellites and fiber feeds [2.93], creating a "free" intercontinental television feed—the modern-day equivalent of World War II short-wave news feeds across oceans. And satellite telephone video, albeit fuzzy for now, is a staple of networks' international news coverage.

Inexpensive global news will become increasingly routine, dropping the business barrier to entry to a level where the smallest local television news organization can perform easily on a global stage.

3. EMPOWER AND ENCOURAGE VIEWER-PRODUCED REPORTING. Millions of Internet users have become accustomed to creating content, much of it related to

news. And there are many examples throughout the world of organized or loosely confederated reporting, whether through such groups as the Silver Stringers [2.94], senior citizens who began to use early Web creation tools from MIT to create their own online news service, or through weblogs that are proliferating throughout professional journalism and, even more so, the general Internet community. There are even weblog index sites, such as the blogdex [2.95], an index of weblog links, which by 2003 was surveying 14,000 weblogs and their links every day, according to its developer, Cameron Marlow. [2.96] (The explosion of blogs preceded the creation of podcasting and RSS feeds; see Part V, below.)

In Europe, there are striking examples of audience empowerment: The Italian daily newspaper *La Repubblica* now has 1,000 schools linked to its Web site, the most outreach any news organization has done with schools, according to Jack Driscoll, editor-in-residence at MIT Media Laboratory (see 2.3.1, above).

Deborah Potter cited examples of audience-produced journalism at National Public Radio and at WHYY-FM in Philadelphia [2.97]. Potter also said she posted a television documentary on her Web site that could be taken apart and reassembled by viewers online. However, these experiments were on radio or on the Internet, not on television.

But in the U.K., the BBC has taken audience empowerment to its logical end: The network has been experimenting with "Open Centers" in the middle of towns that train residents to use e-mail and the Internet—and to shoot and edit video [2.98]. Viewers also can drop in to check their e-mail, just as at a public library. For viewers who prefer training closer to home, the BBC has a fleet of twelve "Mobile Zone" mobile IT classrooms [2.99], "so rural communities are not excluded," according to the BBC's Nigel Kay. The fleet's bus drivers double as new-media instructors, and all of the buses are equipped to originate live broadcasts.

"These projects are instrumental and linked one way or another," said Nigel Kay, who runs BBC local newscasts.

Now, video from viewers in Hull is a regular feature on the BBC Web site, and audio versions are broadcast on BBC Radio. Kay said the best video from nonprofessional viewers is starting to appear on BBC broadcast television, in local newscasts and in breaks between programs. [2.100]

"It's quite unlike conventional reporting, but quite compelling," he said, adding viewer-produced stories "challenge our journalists on what news is."

The new mission, according to Kay, is "getting closer to audiences," especially audiences that have historically watched more of Britain's commercial channels and less of the BBC, viewers described by Kay as "poorer, black and Asian."

"We are empowering the audience," said Richard Sambrook, who also viewed the local news initiative as helping to fulfill the BBC's "educational role." And the audience in Hull has embraced the new service: The BBC was underperforming in Hull, according to Sambrook, but after the changes, the number of BBC viewers in Hull "shot up."

Now, "Open Center" BBC community access offices are opening across the U.K., all operated with local educational authorities, according to Kay, and they will be introduced at BBC regional radio stations around the U.K. as the stations are refurbished. That local radio link was key, said Kay, who once ran the BBC's regional Radio Sheffield station.

"There's no reason the stations [in the U.S.] can't do that," said Marty Haag. "You're really getting this down to the level of people. That's marvelous."

"Let parents shoot kids' sports and plays," said Bill Kovach. "Or let high school kids shoot their own events. Let them get a toehold in journalism." Kovach also suggested finding neighborhoods' storytellers, perhaps at assisted-living homes, and "let them tell their stories."

"We have 'America's Funniest Home Videos,' " noted Ulrich Neumann, director of USC's Integrated Media Systems Center [2.101]. "Why not 'America's Best Video News'?"

The key, of course, is to engage and empower the audience while retaining the essence, values and standards of journalism. Mark Thalhimer, senior project director of the RTNDA Future of News Project [2.102], said viewer-produced video could be a way of injecting informed commentary into local news. Viewer-produced video could be used, he said, to include people with significant expertise but limited video skills—say, a professor from the University of Houston or a doctor from the Stanford Medical Center—to contribute regularly to a local news service.

2.4 <u>Medium-term opportunities</u>

1. EXPERIMENT WITH NEW FORMS OF LOCAL NEWS. The BBC's Nigel Kay said he and his colleagues have spent "a great deal of time" looking at local television newscasts in the U.S. He said they found the American newscasts more polished and with better production than local TV news in Europe. Nevertheless, he said it's all looking a bit stale.

"Every other genre [on TV] is constantly reinventing itself," said Kay, but not local television news, which he described as essentially the same as in the 1970s.

"We have lost our monopoly on the means of production, and we have lost our monopoly on the means of distribution," Kay said, pointing to desktop video and distribution via the Internet. Those tools, he noted, are now available—and affordable—"to charities, lobbies, the self-interested." Journalists have lost control of the high-end means of production, so non-journalists could be the innovators, reinventing information and grabbing attention from those pledged to standards and ethics.

"If we [journalists] don't do it, there is no reason someone else won't do it," Kay warned.

2. NEWS ON DEMAND. The natural evolution of "appointment" local news at 6 and 11—and of the 24-hour local news channels—is to on-demand local news, where the news starts whenever a viewer wants it—and stops, pauses or rewinds whenever a viewer wants it.

Time Warner Cable began offering entertainment and selected news on demand in test markets including New York City in 2003 as a premium (higher-priced) service, the forerunner of a broader on-demand system [2.103]. As the "Moore's Law" [2.104] price-performance curve of computer power renders the cost progressively lower, on-demand video services will become lower in price and spread to a large part of the audience. Instead of "Tune in at 6," it will be, "Set your news tuner to NBC4."

But these are not mechanical wheels set in motion to play back a recorded newscast, as if the viewer had taped the news on a VCR. Instead, new forms of news on demand would be computer-based services. This could offer opportunities to bundle micro-local news stories with metro-wide newscasts. For example, the KNBC-TV "NBC4" newscast seen in Culver City would be different from the "NBC4" newscast seen across town in Hollywood—perhaps with different partners in each neighborhood providing different levels of micro-local news and community information. One issue will be whether on-demand video diffuses as a function of household income, as some technologies have, or whether it follows cell phones and Play Station video game technologies and diffuses across income levels.

3. TV NEWS ON CELL PHONES. Television pictures with picture quality acceptable to viewers now can be transmitted by satellite telephones, as viewers of the 2003 Iraq war coverage

know well. And the declining price of sat phones—down to $3,000 in a few years—will make the telephone an economically compelling replacement for local and network news remote trucks. Even from Iraq, a video feed can cost as little as $6 per minute. And network news crews are shooting and editing video on "pro-sumer" digital video cameras and laptop-based edit systems straight from the shelves of consumer stores. This strongly suggests the waning days of such familiar equipment as large cameras and satellite uplink trucks.

"This won't replace what we have in the driveway," said John Miller, news director of CBS-owned KTVT-TV in Dallas [2.105], "but it could replace the next one." Instead of spending $1 million for one more satellite truck, Miller said he could spend less money and provide a satellite phone to equip every camera crew in his newsroom.

But consider the next step: Video cell phones are already a fad among teenagers in other parts of the world, and their arrival is imminent for U.S. consumers. In Korea, teenagers watch music videos on their cell phones, and Finland is transmitting digital television programs in a cell-phone-friendly format. [2.106] This technology could have a more powerful impact on local television news than camcorders and $3,000 sat phones. If you can watch the news on your cell phone—and e-mail your own cell phone's video to friends, or to a local television newsroom [2.107]—this becomes audience involvement on a hitherto unimagined scale [2.108].

But cell phones are just one possible extrapolation of today's "lipstick" cameras. Live video via cell phone could be the next iteration of the photo cell phone [2.109]. Or we could see wristwatch-style devices, as envisioned by Bill Gates [2.110], or 360-degree transmitter-receivers built into eyeglasses, as John Pavlik has tested at Columbia University [2.111]. But Gates' designs and other proprietary structures raise issues of editorial control in closed-access systems [2.112].

One way or another, the democratization of gathering and editing video is poised to take a huge leap by the end of the decade, with an interesting ancillary question of whether the aesthetics of high-end video will be as affected as it has been by the advent of camcorders. But whatever the aesthetic, the impact on news, including and especially local news, could be considerable, with the rise of "citizen journalism."

"I think that's absolutely inevitable," said John Markoff, who covers technology for *The New York Times* [2.113]. But he said we already have seen glimpses of what this future may be.

"As usual, the science fiction guys got there first," Markoff explained. "Let's see, there's 'Max Headroom' [2.114] the British television show that sort of outlined that world, and I think there have been a number of other science fiction guys who've written about a world like that. That goes back to David Gelernter's *Mirror Worlds* [2.115] idea, in which he argued that the networking of the world would inevitably mean that everything is instrumented. In that kind of a world, I think one of the things that does for journalism is it sort of changes our role in ways that I find totally baffling at this moment." Of course a fully instrumented world, where everything is pre-indexed and sorted, is still at least a few years in the future.

4. IM AND CHAT. Millions, especially young people, already use online chat and Instant Messenger to comment on programs while they are watching. Local television news could encourage and coordinate simultaneous chat alongside news, perhaps even incorporating it into content in the manner of CNN's "Talk Back Live." Sometimes this becomes of journalistic significance, as when *The New York Times* published excerpts from simultaneous chat by people watching television coverage of the space shuttle Columbia disaster [2.116].

5. NEW TECHNOLOGIES FOR EDITING AND SELECTION. Developers at news organizations such as CBS

News and at research labs at MIT and elsewhere are planning for the routine embedding of geo-referencing tags on all video and perhaps all still images. This means editors (or anyone else) will be able to search the library or the Internet for all images of a certain place on earth. [2.117] And it means viewers can request all television news stories from a certain spot—say, within a certain radius of their homes. It also will enable anyone to contribute geo-referenced images, whether tagging pictures they have taken themselves or attaching tags to historic images, such as the test project "Image Maps," tagging and scanning vintage photographs of Cambridge, Massachusetts. [2.118]

6. NEW TECHNOLOGIES FOR LOCATING INFOR-MATION. Researchers for decades have pursued the artificial intelligence Holy Grail of plain English inquiries, but some now claim to be close to their goal. One is the MIT Media Laboratory, home of the Open Mind project [2.119], which the Lab's director said has made significant progress.

"It tries to use some common sense to express a naive search in a more sophisticated way," said Walter Bender, executive director of the Media Lab [2.120]. "My favorite pet example is if you type into Google, 'I want help getting rid of the mice in my kitchen,' then somewhere there is pest control in Cambridge, but certainly not on the first page. Open Mind says [to itself] 'help with mice' equals 'pest control.' " But Bender did not claim Open Mind or its sister projects are ready for prime time—yet.

7. NEW TECHNOLOGIES FOR NEWS GATHERING. Network news has used space-based remote sensing and satellite imagery for years to show "denied" areas, such as North Korea or Iran. [2.121] And local television newscasts have used helicopter-mounted infrared sensors for spot news coverage at night. These technologies are becoming progressively less expensive, bringing them within the reach of small-market

and micro-local newscasts. [2.122] But these are just the start: Consider techniques that are in the labs or in the field, such as Through-Wall Imaging, demonstrated at the FCC in 2003, which does exactly what its name suggests [2.123]. As with remote sensing, eavesdropping and false pretenses, old-fashioned ethics will once again be confronted with newfangled tools.

2.5 Long-term opportunities

1. EXTRAPOLATIONS FROM 2003. The march of Moore's Law [2.104] will lead to ever smarter computer-based "receivers," which we may still call "television sets." And digital television channels and the oversupply of fiber will lead, at least for a while, to a relaxation of spectrum scarcity. What does this offer to journalism?

—Local television digital channels now coming into use can be split into five or six simultaneous video program feeds—and that is just within its FCC-licensed band. As compression advances, ever more "channels" can be squeezed into the same space. "Zoned" editions and micro-local news services could be transmitted live using over-the-air digital multiplexing and WiFi distribution platforms or on a slightly delayed "on-demand" service.

—The falling price of video, video editing and video transmission will lead to a flood of content. Just think of the bored motel attendant in the Qwest television advertisement, who said, "We have every movie ever made, in every language, any time, night or day." [2.124] How will editors navigate this flood? How will the audience?

"Memory prosthesis" devices are being developed to help our pre-digital brains cope with the digital deluge, and the design and use of these technologies could have a profound impact on news and information as it is gathered and stored. One approach being developed at MIT lets users tag information by laughing, or by correlated galvanic skin response. The highest response usually indicates high interest, while the lowest, according to researchers, may mean you have fallen asleep [2.125], while another changes the color of room lights when "important" information becomes available. One example from local news: Construction has closed your street again.

All of this will require major changes in the late-20th-century business model used by almost every local station.

"The financial model is the key to a lot of this," said Miller, "and until the media companies learn to think differently about how they get paid, it's going to be really difficult for them to support these new broadcast distribution schemes, because they can't get the profit margins they are getting now. Instead of 20% margins, you might have to settle for 3% — of a much larger gross. But [in the short run], shareholders won't stand for it."

2. THE GRAMMAR OF REALITY. "Television is all about experience," says Deborah Potter at NewsLab training sessions, and as a veteran of organizing seminars on future formats she knows the field in detail. [2.126] Early 360-degree wraparound television pictures have been in prototypes for years, with some Internet transmissions of wraparound views of sports events.

But these are the first early glimpses of what will soon be commonplace: Turner Broadcasting was planning to introduce a customized 360-degree format to record action throughout a full basketball court or a NACSAR race track, according to USC's Ulrich Neumann. That would give television directors access to video of the entire arena or field, not just the "cut" version that aired live, enabling them to choose replay angles after the action is over.

Immersive media formats that will enable viewers to see in 3-D and, more important in many ways, to *hear* in 3-D, without goggles or earphones, are being developed. One such technology was demonstrated in 2002, transmitting a symphony concert from Florida to California [2.127]. These formats are expected to be available in consumer devices by 2007–2010, with remote immersive experiential transmissions compressed to well within the bandwidth of a current television "channel."

But how do you "edit" experiential news? What is the grammar of reality?

Then there is the matter of ethics: Today, seeing is believing, even if we know better. With immersive news, you will have been there and experienced the news story, been in the refugee camp, been at the political convention, been on the streets of Baghdad. But as with video, immersive formats are digital bits —and equally subject to manipulation. In the 1980s we saw the first synthetic video, fake news events indistinguishable from live television (remember the 1978 movie "Capricorn One," and its depiction of a realistic faked Mars landing). In the 2010s if not before, we will experience fake experiences.

PART III: LOCAL RADIO NEWS – FOR SOME, THE FUTURE IS NOW

It seemed to me that if radio could broadcast the news of the day and special events, it would be a highly desirable service to the more serious listeners. In return, those listeners would appreciate radio —and particularly CBS—for giving them more thoughtful fare than just entertainment.

—William S. Paley, *As It Happened* [3.1]

3.1 Background

In the 1930s, when William Paley and other pioneers invented broadcast news, radio was the king of media. Seventy years later, radio is in many ways the Rodney Dangerfield medium: It gets no respect.

But radio is thriving. And radio news is thriving, with high percentages of listeners giving local stations high marks for news and information, according to a 2003 Zogby survey [3.2]. However, listeners also say they do not trust radio news as much as television news or newspapers, according to a 2000 survey for the Radio-Television News Directors Association [3.3].

As music stations have dropped most or all of their newscasts, radio news broadcasts are heard on only a handful of stations in each city: Most areas still have one successful commercial all-news station, and a few big cities, such as New York and Los Angeles, have two. They have been joined by Spanish-language all-news stations in some cities.

In addition, most areas also have at least one commercial news-talk station, programming news in peak audience morning and afternoon "drive time" and telephone call-in, talk and sports during midday and evening hours.

These program forms swept across the country in the 1960s, when modern commercial all-news radio was invented by Westinghouse at WINS in New York City and then adopted by rival CBS for all of its AM stations. Boosted by such major stories as the 1965 Northeast blackout and historic blizzards a few years later, all-news radio climbed to the top of the audience ratings, using a format that relied on unwavering predictability.

"All-news has to be a utility, like a faucet or a light switch," explained Jim Farley, an editor at WINS in its early all-news days and now vice president for news and programming at WTOP, the all-news station in Washington, D.C. [3.4] "The listener turns on all-news radio and news comes out of the speaker, news in the same format, 24 hours a day."

By the mid-1970s, all-news was such a success that CBS encouraged all of its affiliated AM stations to adopt an all-news or news-talk format. So while Westinghouse focused on locally oriented all-news stations in New York, Los Angeles, Chicago and Philadelphia, CBS Radio was offering national advertisers a nationwide chain of all-news stations—and a nationwide upscale all-news audience.

When Westinghouse bought CBS, almost all of the big-city all-news stations in the United States were brought under a single owner, now Viacom, which even owns both competing all-news stations in the largest cities, such as New York and Los Angeles. All-news continues to draw a large number of mainly older listeners, as well as the banks, airlines and car dealers who want to reach the upscale audiences that listen to all-news stations.

News-talk predated all-news, and such legendary stations as WOR in New York and WGN in Chicago were local institutions as far back as five, six and seven decades ago. Today, just as Viacom owns or is affiliated with all-news stations around the country, leading news-talk stations in the largest markets are owned by Disney, which is affiliated with others around the country through its ABC Radio subsidiary.

After all but monopolizing the network radio business in the early 20th century, NBC abandoned radio entirely in the mid-1980s, selling off its radio network and owned stations and closing its NBC News radio services, including the continuous 24-hour all-news NBC NIS (News and Information Service).

Also in the mid-1980s, the audience for news and public affairs on public radio stalled after a decade of growth (NPR's audience actually declined in 1986). But public radio news has grown in listeners and support since then, as the network and the stations strengthened their national and local news and public affairs services

Much of the growth can be credited to the creation of new news-talk formats at public radio stations. Building on NPR's national morning and afternoon drive-time newsmagazines, "Morning Edition" and "All Things Considered," local public stations dropped music programming, typically classical music or jazz, to add local interview and call-in programs. By 1990, many general managers and program directors at NPR music stations were concerned that serious music would migrate from FM to improved CD-quality sound available via new technologies (including satellite radio, just on the drawing boards then); with the national programs as a foundation, they saw an opportunity to create new public affairs formats. To many, San Francisco stations were the template.

KQED-FM in San Francisco was one of the first major public stations to eliminate music entirely and convert to news-talk, in 1986. Facing two strong commercial news stations in San Francisco, CBS' KCBS-AM and ABC's KGO-AM, KQED differentiated itself with in-depth coverage of significant local issues, just as NPR's newsmagazines featured longer-form national coverage. At that time, stories could run as long as 20 minutes on "All Things Considered" (more recently the format was changed to halve that maximum length). San Francisco's municipally owned NPR station, KALW-FM, also had an all-public affairs format, with NPR newsmagazines supplemented by documentaries and diverse spoken-word programming, so San Francisco suddenly had four sources of serious radio news —and all were successful. [3.5]

By the end of the 20th century, NPR news was the financial cash cow that supported the music and performance programming and the rest of the public radio program service. And on commercial stations, radio news was increasingly available only on a few all-news and news-talk stations in each city, which were highly profitable. NPR news and the traditional commercial all-news stations may be all the journalism that survives on radio in the near future, according to such industry observers as Jim Russell, who helped start "Morning Edition" and other NPR News programs before moving to run "Marketplace." [3.6]

Commercial all-news programming has remained unchanged for decades; the last major commercial all-news innovation was the "22-minute format" introduced at KFWB and WINS in the early 1970s—because, as one all-news station manager said, "I run the No. 1 billing [advertising sales] station in the market. Why should I change?"

3.2 All-news AM radio focuses on local service

Commercial all-news stations, almost all on the AM band, focus relentlessly on local service information: weather, traffic, sports, and above all, the time.

The first all-news stations in the 1960s featured a "clock" that is still with us: sports at :15 and :45 after the hour, business at :25 and :55, service information every seven minutes ("Traffic and weather eight times every hour"). But programmers soon found it was highly promotable to run service information every ten minutes, "on the ones" (:01, :11, :21, :31, :41 and :51 after the hour) for locally focused all-news stations, such as KFWB and WINS, or "on the eights" (:08, :18, :28, and so forth) for stations carrying network CBS News on the hour.

Research also showed that giving the time, often, was essential, especially in the morning. Anchors were instructed to give the time every three minutes most of the day, and as frequently as every minute.

Local news was scheduled just as carefully. Research consistently showed listeners preferred local news to world and national news, unless there was a war or national emergency. And if the content was divided evenly between local and national news, listeners perceived the local news to be far less than half; only when stations broadcast more local news did listeners find the balance even, according to early research conducted by Westinghouse Broadcasting, which then owned WINS and KFWB. Anecdotal evidence indicates local governments were covered more extensively by local radio than by local television.

As more AM stations converted to all-news and news-talk, ABC News and CBS News increased their radio production to provide more national coverage in forms that stations could integrate easily into local news and news-talk formats. This meant more 60-second reports, which stations preferred for fast-paced programming. For major breaking national news stories, it meant more live coverage. For its all-news and news-talk stations, CBS News began producing "instant" specials on breaking news that were in four- and five-minute segments, spread over an entire day or weekend. But always the focus was on local news and service, because that was where stations thrived—and sold commercials.

In the 1970s, the networks tried to appeal to audiences with more national news. NBC began its national News and Information Service, a 24-hour all-news radio program service that enabled affiliates to convert to all-news while programming as little as ten minutes per hour of local news. NBC would fill the rest. NBC failed to attract powerful AM stations and eventually ended the service. At about the same time, CBS News piloted a long-form radio news service that would have enabled the dozens of CBS all-news and news-talk stations to fill more overnight and weekend hours with live national news and features. CBS never launched its service, which was in some ways rendered moot by the rise of long-form national news at the low, left end of the FM band—the noncommercial radio stations.

3.3 **Public radio focuses on local community**

Public radio news from the start was conceived as a national radio news service, because public stations could not afford to hire the substantial staff of anchors, editors, writers and reporters that commercial all-news and news-talk stations employed. "All Things Considered" and then "Morning Edition" and "Weekend Edition" were multi-hour national network newsmagazines with only one to three minutes for local news headlines. But stations soon discovered they could increase their audience between the long-form NPR magazines with locally originated long-form public affairs, two-hour interview and telephone call-in programs, which stations could produce almost as inexpensively as classical music and jazz programs.

Public radio stations had found a popular and even lucrative niche, reaching an increasing number of listeners and attracting more money from listener donations and from corporate underwriters. But they still never competed with the commercial all-news stations in local news and service. Instead, station managers and news directors began to experiment with new forms of community-based reporting. One of the leaders is Minnesota Public Radio [3.7], best known around the country for "Prairie Home Companion" [3.8] and other national programming. MPR operates a statewide network that is one of the most successful public radio groups in the U.S. MPR started Public Radio International (originally American Public Radio) [3.9], and now it is branching into other parts of the country.

MPR's West Coast center is at KPCC-FM in Pasadena, California, [3.10] where MPR has built the entire news service around community-level coverage of the sprawling Los Angeles metropolitan area.

"We are all about community and communities," said Paul Glickman, KPCC's news director [3.11]. "It is very much our agenda to connect the many and disparate communities." Formerly NPR's foreign editor, Glickman conceded his reporters cover a large area. But instead of abandoning micro-local news coverage, as Los Angeles television stations have done, KPCC uses community coverage both for news and for the station's identity.

"Our coverage area is quite large, a vast area," he said, but added, "Our radio station is a virtual community meeting place. Our goal is to make this place a centering institution. Through the miracle of radio, we bring together South Los Angeles with Little Saigon. That's very much what we're about."

Glickman said that means story selection has to be carefully calibrated.

"We have to be more selective," he explained. "They [KPCC stories] need to resonate with people and the area. The best local news stories are universal and resonate."

"We edit and structure stories to generalize," added Anthea Raymond Beckler, KPCC's senior news editor [3.12]. A story on housing in Long Beach should be recognizable to a listener in Norwalk.

But with all of the attention on community news, KPCC still must cover the major "institutional" local news each day, the news conferences and spot news stories that are the staple of typical local newscasts. And that means there is always pressure on reporters—and from reporters—to cover more stories.

"We feel it a lot," Beckler said. "It's there on the daybook. They [newsmakers] say something every day."

"We're a news station," said Glickman. "We have to give people the news. We can't ignore it."

And Beckler said many reporters prefer to cover "institutional" news.

"They see what their peers are doing," she explained, saying some view covering City Hall as more prestigious than covering communities.

So each day's assignment list represents a balance of micro-local and regional, the City Hall news conference and the grass roots. And grass-roots coverage requires more resources.

"It's more time-consuming, labor-intensive," Glickman explained. "Every day in my nine years at NPR [on the foreign desk] we had that tension: covering official news, or that great feature everyone will remember."

KPCC has expanded its newsroom to cover more community stories and more official news. Starting with one reporter in 2000, the staff has grown to six full-time reporters, augmented by part-time and freelance journalists.

"Over the next four or five years we could have eight or ten reporters," Glickman predicted, adding the larger staff would enable the station to produce more in-depth reporting. "The more people we have, the more leeway we have to cut a person loose for a few days."

The station's community news segments are broadcast as part of the NPR national newsmagazines, and that raises the bar for local reporting: to maintain the same level of reporting and production in KPCC local segments that listeners hear in the national NPR program.

"It has to be seamless, whether it's national, international or local," said Glickman. "The challenge for us is to have such quality that the listener doesn't notice when we switch from the network to a local story."

During the day, between the NPR magazines, KPCC also wants to connect communities, in its interview and discussion programs, and that means live remotes almost every week.

"Another big piece of what we're about is taking talk shows to communities," said Glickman. "Get us out of the studio and into the world."

He said he wanted KPCC to originate live programs from as many communities as it can, and he plans to do more and more live remotes over time. That meant producing a live two-hour talk show from the Queen Mary in Long Beach one week and originating from a community center in Compton the next week. Before each visit, KPCC reporters and researchers identified community issues to discuss and community leaders to invite, in order to incorporate diverse voices and viewpoints from the varied local communities of the Los Angeles area.

Over the summer, KPCC took one of its talk shows on a road trip north along the California coast, looking for issues and stories that "tied back into Southern California." KPCC also was helped by its nightly (later weekly) broadcast of the national "Tavis Smiley Show," [3.13] which is broadcast from predominantly minority South Los Angeles. Smiley's guest list includes a who's who of African-American political leaders and entertainers, and it has become the fastest-growing program on public radio.

Since KPCC began focusing on communities three years ago, the station has won major awards—and the station's audience has doubled. In 2003, KPCC won 12 Los Angeles Press Club Awards, more than any other radio station in Southern California. KPCC also won first and second place in the Radio Journalist of the Year category. [3.14]

"People are noticing," said Glickman, pointing to steady growth in listeners from 200,000–250,000 in 2000 to more than 400,000 in the spring of 2003.

But he said none of that growth has come at the expense of the other NPR public affairs station serving Los Angeles, KCRW in Santa Monica. KCRW, which broadcasts "Morning Edition" and "All Things Considered" along with KPCC, also added 200,000 new listeners in the past three years, according to Glickman.

Public radio gained a net total of 400,000 new listeners in Los Angeles in three years, a trend Kevin Klose, president of National Public Radio, described as "phenomenal."

Other public radio stations have found audiences growing as they added community-level coverage. And "connect" and "connection" have become among the words most used by public radio station managers around the U.S.

"What I'm seeing is a trend going up," said Susan Clampitt, general manager and executive director of WAMU Radio, the NPR news-talk station in Washington, D.C. [2.53] "There is a thirst for community. People can connect, get involved and find out what's going on and get a sense of place and community."

Clampitt said she wanted to cover Washington residents who were not in the news, what she called "the Washington nobody knows about." That includes low-income areas, but also retirement communities, young people (see "Teen Voices," described in "Reconnecting With Younger Audiences," 2.2.4 above) and the arts community, all of which, she said, are not often covered.

"Washington is the choral capital of the United States," explained Clampitt, who was at the National Endowment for the Arts before joining WAMU. "Theater [in Washington] is second only to New York" in the number of seats. While other stations focused on crime, politics and institutional news, she saw an opportunity to focus on communities, "the other Washington" and on culture and arts.

But while KPCC was seeking micro-local stories that resonated throughout Southern California, Clampitt said WAMU wanted to find community stories that could tell global stories.

"How can we use this area as a microcosm of the world?" she asked, and said she found the answer in Washington's fast-growing immigrant communities. Especially on WAMU's long-form interview and telephone programs during the day, micro-local could become global. "We talked to Iraqi Americans on life after 9/11. Immigration is a huge story, so we went to the Bolivian community in Arlington [Virginia]. These stories are America's stories."

The global theme also played out in local arts and culture in Washington, D.C.: Artists from Asia, Africa and Latin America perform to standing-room audiences in the capital's largest theaters without attracting the attention of mainstream media, according to Alicia Adams, vice president of international programming at the John F. Kennedy Center for the Performing Arts. [3.15]

As at KPCC, listeners discovered and liked the new focus. WAMU's audience hit an all-time high in 2003, and listener contributions and corporate underwriting increased 31 % between 2000 and 2002, according to Ruth Thompson, WAMU's senior director of marketing and communications.[3.16]

WAMU and KPCC also were among the handful of public radio stations supporting the start of a new locally oriented news bureau to cover national news from Capitol Hill. Designed to supplement NPR's network news, the new public radio Capitol News Connection launched in 2003 with a mission to make all national news local.

"We live in a very diverse country," explained bureau manager Melinda Wittstock [3.17]. "A single piece on NPR will not reflect that diversity. [We] take a national story and report it differently for different communities. Amtrak is a good example.

People in Arizona don't really care. People in the Northeast really care. Newspapers have done this before, but this is new for public radio."

The goal, said Wittstock, was to ascertain the major issues in each community and then find what was relevant in Washington, D.C. One of the bureau's first stories was an analysis of the energy policies advocated by Representative Frank Lucas, whose Oklahoma district is "the Saudi Arabia of wind power" in America. That was big news in Oklahoma City.

Another early story was a package for KERA in Dallas about healthcare legislation sponsored by Representative Kay Granger, a Texas Republican. She gained the support of Democrat Albert Wynn of Maryland, who then persuaded the Congressional Black Caucus to support Granger's healthcare proposals.

"It was a nice story on how you build coalitions," said Wittstock. It was also a story, she said, that was below the radar screen of national broadcasters, but had a disproportionate impact on north Texas.

The bureau also was designed to help local stations produce their two-hour local interview and discussion programs. If a national question was raised during KPCC's live community talk program, Wittstock said her bureau could get a member of the California House or Senate delegation to a microphone, live, for an answer.

The bureau was supposed to serve no more than ten or fifteen local stations in its first year, according to Wittstock, but double that number want to receive stories, so she has asked for more reporters. And many of these stations are outside the big cities, with midsize and small stations from New England to the South to the Pacific Northwest now defining local community news to include heretofore largely unreported Washington deal-making that affects residents' lives.

"Identify your audience and speak to your audience" was one of the bureau's mottos, she said.

3.4 Bringing radio news to traditional audiences

While public radio news has grown over the past two decades, the commercial all-news format that began in the 1960s remained popular and profitable. One reason was the relatively upscale audience of listeners, which was why such advertisers as banks, airlines and auto makers have long considered all-news a must-buy. Some of those audience characteristics are shared by public radio stations' news programs, which was why public radio news often attracted proportionally more corporate underwriting announcements than music programs on public radio, even if the audience was the same size.

Commercial all-news radio stations also have achieved extraordinary reach, or "cume"—the total number of listeners to the station. WINS in New York routinely advertises itself as the largest "cume" station in the United States. Because most listeners to commercial news stations do not listen for long— far less time than listeners to music stations—the audience of a commercial all-news station at any given moment may well be lower than for a similar music station, as listeners dip in and out of the all-news programming for a quick check of weather or traffic.

Some all-news station managers and news directors maintain this listening pattern has resulted in underestimating the audience for radio news. WTOP's Jim Farley described an exercise conducted by his station, asking people to "write down all the stations you listen to." All-news WTOP often was not listed by its regular listeners. "They said, 'When you said radio stations, I thought you said music stations,' " explained Farley. He noted that exercise mimicked the methodology of the Arbitron audience measurement service that has been the basis for radio ratings—and commercial advertising sales. So to remind listeners they include news in their radio station mix,

Farley said to combat the undercount of radio news listening, he began using a new promotional announcement on WTOP: "Your favorite radio station doesn't play any music."

In the spring of 2003, WTOP went to the top of the radio ratings in Washington, D.C., with a 21 % advantage over the runner-up music station in the peak morning hours and dominating the radio dial "in virtually every category," according to the *Washington Post*. [3.18]

So even by Arbitron measurements, over the course of a day, the total number of listeners who dip in and out of commercial all-news stations can be very, very large. And those large numbers include some demographics that might be a surprise: For example, African-American politicians have long known that one of the most desirable media for their messages is the commercial all-news stations, such as WINS in New York or KYW in Philadelphia. In Los Angeles, members of Representative Maxine Waters' staff viewed all-news KFWB as the most important station to reach her predominantly minority constituents, far more valuable than the Los Angeles stations programmed explicitly for African-American audiences [3.19].

But commercial mass-audience all-news stations may be overly reliant on listeners in cars. Once one of a few sources of solid information in the peak early morning hours, all-news radio has encountered competition from public radio, from 24-hour all-news television networks, from local cable news channels and from local television news, which until recently was not a factor in the early morning hours.

"All-news stations will survive until you can get TV or cable reception in your car," said Farley.

3.5 **Bringing radio news to new audiences**

Without waiting for car televisions, radio stations were expanding their local news services to take advantage of new methods of delivering their programs. Part of that expansion was on radio, sometimes enabled, or forced, by circumstances of marketing and technology: At 1500, WTOP was on the "wrong" band (AM) and the "wrong" end (the lower frequencies are preferred).

"AM, with some exceptions, is a dying band," admitted Farley. "Exceptions are the major-market 'booming' signals [they can be heard for hundreds of miles]—WINS, WCBS, WFAN, WBZ, WGN, WBBM. People have to have more than one reason to go to the AM dial, such as the Yankees baseball on WCBS. AM radio committed hara-kiri. All kinds of people have given up on AM."

The solution at WTOP came from what Farley said was an unexpected source: To fill a gap in WTOP-AM's coverage, WTOP bought a small FM station west of Washington and converted it to WTOP-FM, 107.7. Simulcasting the same programming as the AM station, WTOP-FM found an entirely new audience—an audience all-news station managers thought they had lost forever.

"On 107.7, the average age is ten years younger," said Farley. "They spend all their time on the FM band."

The problem was not that younger listeners did not like all-news stations. The problem was that younger listeners never listen to AM radio. Putting the AM radio programming on an FM transmitter let more younger listeners tune in.

The next expansion of WTOP's audience also was unexpected, according to Farley, but it was not on radio, or at least on radio as most would define the medium. It began when WTOP started posting service information on its Web site, http://www.wtopnews.com/. And Farley said it was not planned. [3.20]

"WTOP was dragged to the Internet by our listeners," he explained. "At 7 a.m. one morning during a snow storm, I opened up my e-mail and discovered we received over a hundred e-mails complaining that the school closings were not online. So we started posting that on our Web site."

Then, according to Farley, frustrated would-be listeners called and asked for audio streaming. Workers in Washington, D.C., office buildings complained they could not hear either the AM or FM signal because of poor reception. The solution: Distribute it live over the Internet, which Farley called "another transmitter downtown." Suddenly workers could listen at work, running WTOP in the background on their office computers.

"There are 100 million radios," he explained. "But everyone now has a computer. It was all driven by them [the audience] because you couldn't listen at work."

He said the Internet streaming costs $10,000 per month, sometimes more for peak listening days when WTOP has to order more bandwidth to meet the demand. Over a year, it's "moderately profitable," according to Farley, despite Arbitron's refusal to include online listeners in WTOP's official audience ratings.

"Arbitron won't give stations credit for listeners on the Internet or on cable TV," he complained. Some stations can be heard over cable television or on closed-circuit talk or music channels, where listening may not be measured by Arbitron. But on the Internet, because of the architecture of online live streaming, WTOP knows exactly how many listeners' computers are logged onto its Web site, so Farley's sales department can share this with advertisers, telling them about the audience that is not included in the ratings report.

Farley said the online audience held another surprise: Just as WTOP-FM added listeners ten years younger than those tuned to the AM station, WTOP on the Internet added another audience that programmers assumed would never listen to all-news radio: radio listeners twenty years younger than those listening to WTOP-AM.

"People listening online are in their 20s and 30s," said Farley, who described the Internet as a way "to let people listen to us." Farley and other radio managers were encouraged by research [3.21] showing streaming on the Internet detracts from television viewing and newspaper reading but does not affect radio listening.

And because the Internet is global, anyone in the world can listen. WTOP has had a huge global boost in its audience, because it is one of the few all-news radio stations in the U.S. that is not owned by Viacom. When Internet audio streaming began, Viacom banned all of its powerful news stations, from KNX and KFWB in Los Angeles to WINS and WCBS in New York, from going online. That left the field open to WTOP, owned by Bonneville, so WTOP's online service became a de facto commercial all-news Voice of America on the Internet. (Viacom later reversed itself and allowed its all-news stations to stream online.)

Success with WTOP online led Farley to add a new Internet-only all-news "radio station," Federal News Radio, an audio service and accompanying Web site [3.22] designed for people who work for the federal government.

Federal News Radio launched with world and national news from the Associated Press, but the unique feature was micro-local news for the community of the federal government, highlighting news that affects government workers. Regular features include updates on pay and benefits for government employees, the latest on U.S. government computers (remember, everyone listens on their computer), the GovBiz Minute (doing business with the government) and the Agency of the Month (think of Charles Kuralt on the road, but touring the federal bureaucracy).

Federal News Radio was profitable the day it launched, according to Farley, because the service was sold out to advertisers weeks and months in advance. By the end of April 2003, Federal News Radio had booked $1.2 million in advertising revenue—

$500,000 more than the total operating cost of FNR for the entire year, according to Farley. Advertising sold over the next eight months would drop down to the bottom line as sheer profit.

"I'd love to buy another AM station," he said, "but none is for sale right now." If he moved FNR to a broadcast station, Farley said, it would be the first time anyone had moved a 24-hour audio program format from the Internet to radio.

Farley said he hoped to build on FNR's success by starting still more Internet-only all-news "radio stations." High on his list was a 24-hour all-news Internet audio service for the U.S. military and a Spanish-language all-news service, all to be tested on the Internet (for a profit) and then possibly brought to a broadcast station. (After this interview, Farley was able to buy another AM station in Washington. Rechristened WFED-AM, the new station now broadcasts FNR over the air.)

Soon WTOP may not need to buy any more broadcast stations to offer FNR and other all-news services over the air. Digital radio technology can fit additional audio signals into existing broadcast bands.

"Everyone is going digital, and stations are having second and third channels," said WAMU's Clampitt.

For example, when WAMU eliminated most of its bluegrass music to make room for more news, it moved the music programs to a new Web site [3.23]. And WGMS-FM, Washington, D.C.'s classical music station, similarly moved its opera and limited-appeal vocal music to a 24-hour Internet site [3.24]. If WAMU and WGMS can accommodate new digital audio channels as well as their existing primary FM signals, bluegrass music and opera could be back on broadcast radio in Washington.

That means WTOP could use extra capacity on its stations to broadcast that military all-news service and Spanish-language local news programming.

Meanwhile, the Internet also has had an effect on the existing local audio news service: WTOP reporters now are asked to file text and photos as well as audio. Visitors entering the newsroom pass a sign reminding everyone about WTOP's photo contest—a photo contest at a radio station.

"All of our reporters have digital cameras," said Farley. "We have the AP photo service, the same top-of-the-line service as TV and newspapers."

And WTOP has started to use video online.

"The Web has given us television," said Farley. "We televise 'Ask the Mayor,'" one of the station's regular call-in programs with elected officials. "And we post 'action information' on the Web site [such as], 'Where can I send a letter to soldiers?' It drives a lot of traffic."

Farley said all-news radio was perfectly positioned to build local online news services, better than television or even a major newspaper, such as the *Washington Post*.

"Radio is a great model on the Web," he said. "Maybe if I tripled my staff to nine or ten, we'd be killing them [the *Post*'s Web site, http://www.washingtonpost.com]."

The biggest cloud on Farley's horizon was what he said was unfair treatment by advertisers, who shun radio news because they believe it appeals mainly to listeners over 55 years old.

"The target [for advertisers] is always 25–54," he explained. "Every year another million people turn 54, and now the baby boomers are the ones turning 54."

According to Farley, auto maker Lexus did research showing listeners over 55 are 11% more likely to buy, but at the Lexus ad agency, "They play the 25–54 game, too." Farley said advertisers only pay for 25- to 54-year-olds, because the rest is a bonus. "They know they can get listeners over 55 for free."

Advertiser pressures are heightened by the demographics of advertising agencies, according to Farley.

"The entry-level job at an ad agency is radio buyer," he said. "The next job up is TV." So radio advertising is purchased by 23- to 25-year-olds, who are among the least likely to listen to radio news.

"They become listeners at age 30, when they have student loans and a mortgage and kids in school. But that's above the age of the buyers."

But at the retail level, where local sales are made, all-news radio stations have been established for decades as stations where listeners are paying close attention.

"We make telephones ring," said Farley. "We'll make your phones ring off the hook." Last winter, WTOP's snow closing announcements were sponsored by a company that sold standby electric power generators.

"They couldn't keep up with the phone calls," Farley said.

3.6 New, uncharted territory for local radio news

1. NEW COMPETITORS ON THE INTERNET. Just as WTOP has developed a national and even international audience for its news streamed over the Internet, thousands of other Internet "radio stations" have launched, most with a tiny fraction of WTOP's budget. So far they have been devoted almost entirely to music and entertainment formats, but it seems inevitable that sooner rather than later, there will be an Internet radio counterpart to Matt Drudge [3.25]. And on the Internet, geography is irrelevant: The radio station that won a 2003 "Best of New York City" competition was an Internet radio station transmitted from a high school in Seattle, Washington. [3.26] The best of New York City was, in fact, created by high school students on the other side of the country. The students' music selection was judged better than anything available from stations in New York City.

Keeping up with technology has always been a challenge. In local radio news, as in many fields, new technology can threaten existing providers and provide an entry point for newcomers.

2. SECONDARY SIGNALS. In many cities, radio listeners can hear PBS "News Hour" on their local public radio station. But in addition, some dashboard car "radios" can already tune in the audio from local television stations, enabling drivers to listen to their favorite soap opera—or local TV news.

Some cars and many home and office radios also are equipped to receive secondary "sideband" stations, which do not appear on most radio receivers. These stations provide local news and entertainment in languages from Korean to Farsi, all below the radar of the mass-media audience ratings. But some non-English-language news was well above the radar: In addition to the enormous audience and commercial success of Spanish-language news, news in Korean has become a mainstay of such AM stations as KYPA in Los Angeles, "Radio Korea" [3.27].

3. DIGITAL RADIO. Digital radio is rapidly approaching. One digital radio music station in the United Kingdom, Kiss 100, attracted almost a million listeners last spring, and two other digital stations reached more than 750,000 listeners apiece. [3.28] Soon this technology will be widespread in the U.S. This will mean hundreds, perhaps thousands, of new radio signals in the U.S., and many more opportunities for local news in years to come.

4. SPREAD-SPECTRUM RADIO. Another new technology, "spread-spectrum" radio, holds the promise of thousands more signals, each one "spread" across a band of frequencies. And of course the Internet, available over the air via WiFi and other wireless access providers, can offer thousands, even millions of "radio" stations.

5. NEW TERRESTRIAL RADIO STATIONS. Meanwhile, a little-noticed patent granted early in 2003 marked the creation of thousands of new local broadcast radio stations in

the U.S., and they are on the air right now. Millions of listeners already tune to them, even if they do not quite know they are tuned to local, not satellite, radio. Here is how it works:

Many new cars now come equipped with radios that receive XM or Sirius radio, two subscription radio services operating in a different set of radio frequencies than AM and FM. Launched in September 2001, XM Radio quickly reached over a million subscribers [3.29] paying a monthly fee similar to cable or satellite television. For their subscription fees, XM and Sirius listeners can select among a hundred channels of news and entertainment, many of them without commercials or funding credits. Radio news available on XM and Sirius is provided by networks including ABC, Fox News Channel, NPR, CNN in English and Spanish and the BBC World Service, also in English and Spanish.

XM and then Sirius offered listeners world and national news, but no local news or weather. Listeners probably assumed satellite radio could deliver only national radio networks, because they assumed they were listening to national feeds coming from XM and Sirius via satellite. But neither assumption was entirely correct.

Drivers listening to XM radio on city streets were "most likely" receiving the signals over a network of more than 700 terrestrial XM transmitters, not from the XM satellites, according to Richard Michalski, XM's director of systems engineering [3.30]. XM terrestrial transmitters blanket major cities in the U.S., to guarantee coverage in urban areas where tall buildings can block signals from the satellites. As of May, 2003 XM had a network of "seven or eight hundred" local radio transmitters around the U.S., according to Michalski. To cover Washington, D.C., XM installed more than 20 transmitters, spread across the District, Maryland and Virginia. The National Association of Broadcasters, which opposed XM's network of terrestrial broadcast facilities, claimed "over 60" XM transmitters covered Boston [3.31].

Each of those transmitters has more than 100 micro-local radio stations playing the same 100 national radio networks, the same programming as the two XM satellites—for now. Each terrestrial transmitter also has up to 20 spare radio channels, or "stations," which XM reserved for as-yet-unannounced new programming. The XM terrestrial transmitters operate on different frequencies from the nationwide satellites. So if an XM radio was tuned to, say, CNN, what actually happened inside the radio receiver was a sampling of which signal was stronger— the satellite or the nearby terrestrial relay station—and the radio would automatically switch to the stronger signal.

The terrestrial transmitters are all monitored from XM's master control room in Washington, just as the satellite channels are. So, using this configuration, XM could insert local news, sports, weather and other programming on its hundreds of local radio transmitters, providing direct competition to the AM and FM radio stations in every major city in the United States. And since XM could direct news or traffic to a specific transmitter serving a particular neighborhood, XM could deliver micro-local information that features only the news or traffic in that neighborhood.

"We have a patent on a way to do that," Michalski said, "and we have an agreement with the FCC not to do that."

According to XM's patent application, XM planned to use its network for "geographically targeted broadcast data, such as weather, sports scores, advertisements and the like." This could be especially attractive as XM's digital service competes with new terrestrial digital stations [3.32].

If this service were activated, the XM network could also enable each listener to select the neighborhood news he or she wanted to hear. Since all programming would be fed via the two XM satellites, said Michalski, if XM transmits local traffic reports for, say, New York, then any listener in the country who wanted to hear New York City traffic reports could tune in to them. That might not be useful for listeners in Seattle, but those headed to Manhattan from New Jersey might want to know which highway to use to approach the city.

Currently, most General Motors cars with XM radio receivers (GM is an investor in XM) also have onboard navigation systems linked to global positioning satellite systems, so the receiver always "knows" where it is, to within a few hundred yards, anywhere in the U.S. Michalski declined to comment on whether that capability could be used to switch among regional or even micro-local terrestrial transmitters—or to deliver locally "zoned" commercials, extending XM's limited commercial inventory to serve local advertisers.

But to program these hundreds of local transmitters with local news, XM would be required either to invest a substantial sum to start local news departments all around the United States or to affiliate with a partner that already had that capability. As it turns out, XM already has just such a partner, the largest radio station group in the United States, Clear Channel Worldwide [3.33].

Clear Channel operates "approximately 1,225" radio stations across the United States, according to its Web site [3.34]. While Clear Channel has been criticized for replacing local music hosts with programs hosted by "dee jays" in remote cities, the company has also leveraged its local presence to extend its reach into local news and information.

For example, on October 21, 2003, Clear Channel announced it would launch digitally transmitted local "traffic information and other locally focused messages" on its stations in each of the 50 largest U.S. cities "by the end of November," 2003. [3.35] All that would be required for XM and Clear Channel to begin broadcasting local or micro-local news, weather and traffic is an adjustment of the XM license by the Federal Communications Commission.

This has alarmed some terrestrial broadcasters, including the broadcasters' industry association, the National Association of Broadcasters.

"We are astonished to learn that XM Radio has secretly acquired a patent that will allow the company to provide local radio programming through its extensive terrestrial repeater network," said Edward O. Fritts, president and CEO of the National Association of Broadcasters. "This development indicates that the FCC International Bureau has either dropped the ball, or that XM believes it does not have to play by the rules. Regardless, XM's lack of candor suggests it is time for Chairman Powell and the individual FCC commissioners to put a halt to this ruse of a terrestrial repeater network." [3.36]

This may become an issue in other countries, as well: XM satellite signals, licensed only to serve the United States, also carry into other countries. And Clear Channel has an equity interest in hundreds of radio stations outside the United States, according to its Web site.

For example, XM's satellite signals extend 400 miles into Mexico, according to Michalski, who added XM even had a listener in Panama. XM satellite signals also can be received north of the border, well into Canada, where Michalski said there is a lively "gray market" of illegal XM radio receivers. Those might soon be legal receivers; XM and Sirius have received permission to begin serving Canada. But public hearings on licenses for Canadian service were scheduled for fall, 2005 to solicit public input. [3.37]

"We're talking to them," said Michalski. Asked about Canadian content rules, which require a certain amount of programming be produced by Canadians, Michalski noted XM had a large percentage of music performed by Canadian musicians.

And to serve Canadian cities, XM would want to install more terrestrial transmitters, each of which can transmit 120 radio stations. Ultimately, XM and Clear Channel could provide micro-local news, weather, traffic, sports—and of course advertising—to cities and micro-local neighborhoods from Canada to the north to Panama to the south.

This could represent significant new competition to existing AM and FM radio stations. It also could represent new opportunities for local radio news, perhaps in partnership with existing news organizations or with other community institutions. Just as the growth of FM radio provided a platform for the growth of local and national public radio news, the extension of the XM band into local broadcasting could provide platforms for new and innovative local public service broadcasting.

PART IV: LOCAL NEWS ON THE INTERNET

The Web is more a social creation than a technical one. I designed it for a social effect—to help people work together—and not as a technical toy. The ultimate goal of the Web is to support and improve our weblike existence in the world. We clump into families, associations and companies. We develop trust across the miles and distrust around the corner. What we believe, endorse, agree with and depend on is representable and, increasingly, represented on the Web.

—Tim Berners-Lee, *Weaving the Web* [4.1]

4.1 Introduction

By the start of the 21st century, Tim Berners-Lee's vision was largely in place: The Internet and the World Wide Web had become a significant and increasingly important source of news, information and community.

By the end of 2003, online news had drawn even with public television and the Sunday morning network news programs as a source of political information in the U.S., according to a 2003 survey by the Pew Research Center [4.2]. And low-income Californians were just as likely as affluent residents to go online for certain categories of news and information, such as health information, according to another 2003 Pew survey [4.3].

With the rise of Internet-delivered news, many television and radio stations have inaugurated online editions of their local news coverage.   Some television newsrooms have integrated broadcast and online (see 2.2.7 "Interactivity," above). And one all-news radio station has had singular editorial and financial success by embracing online technologies (see "Bringing Radio News to New Audiences," 3.5 above). There are also interesting experiments by broadcasters; note the BBC's online local components in 2.2.6 and 2.3.3, above.

However, for the most part, the most widely used news sources online are either aggregators, such as Yahoo or AOL, which have small or no editorial operations of their own, instead collecting the reporting and editing of others; partners of well known broadcast networks, such as CNN.com, MSNBC.com and BBC.co.uk; or sites of national newspapers, such as nytimes.com and Washingtonpost.com, according to 2003 Alexa data. [4.4]

But for local news, the most widely used online sources are almost always the Web site of the dominant daily newspaper. Most of these emerged in the 1990s, often as a defensive measure, as publishers feared Microsoft or other competitors were beginning to pursue the heart of newspaper revenue, especially real estate and help-wanted advertising. [4.5] Sites run by local television and radio stations, as a rule, reached fewer people than newspaper sites, according to Alexa data. [4.6]

By 2000, with the start of the slide in technology stocks and other securities, newspaper Web sites had reached a point of momentary maturity. The voluminous reporting of the daily newspaper was made available free to readers on the Internet, typically with some updating during the day from the Associated Press and other syndicated sources.

4.2 Local service produces local profits

Some newspaper sites, however, have had aggressive development efforts, on the editorial, technical and advertising fronts, that suggest a model of increased public service on the Internet can lead to significant increases in circulation and earnings. One site of interest is in San Diego, California, where SignOnSanDiego.com, the Web site of the daily *Union Tribune* newspaper, has been among the most active in the country experimenting with new ways to serve and reach local audiences.

1. HOW THE SITE IS PRODUCED. Launched in 1995, the site is produced by a total staff of 70, of which one-third are support and advertising. One reason that staff is smaller than those at many other newspaper Web sites was that there were never any corporate personnel, according to Chris Jennewein, who ran the site, with the title Internet operations director [4.7].

"If there's any corporate, it's me," said Jennewein, highlighting the absence of senior managers and administrators.

The heart of the editorial operation has expanded into "a small newsroom" with a sixteen-person breaking news desk, according to the person in charge of news, SignOnSanDiego. com content manager Ron James [4.8]. That number does not include such specialty sections as the four-person arts and entertainment unit. The news staff was drawn from print and broadcast newsrooms, with an emphasis on journalism rather than Web design. And most important, according to James, he can borrow from other departments to supplement the core news staff when he has major news events to cover.

2. EDITORIAL ROUTINE. The site is updated every two hours, from 6 a.m. into early evening, even if there are no major breaking stories. Many of the updates are preprogrammed features and service items. So the daily editorial rundown, "The Sheet," typically starts each day with the instruction "Push the Button"—to launch the preprogrammed 6 a.m. start-of-the-day feature stories.

As with many Web sites, SignOnSanDiego's audience peaks during the business day. But because of readers in other parts of the country, Jennewein said there was an overlay of the business days in the Eastern and Central time zones, with traffic starting to increase sharply at 6 a.m. Pacific time—9 a.m. in the East—and drop off starting at 2 p.m. Pacific time, the end of the business day in the East and Midwest.

"Real-time feedback is important and different," said Jennewein. "Everyone in the site can see the real-time stats showing what pages are being viewed."

For example, when editors saw that a story on health hazards in imported green onions was consistently one of the most widely read stories every hour, they kept it on the home page all day—with updates.

Statistics and usage charts for the site are posted in the newsroom, and some are even posted online. [4.9] Jennewein also proudly handed out copies of current Media Audit [4.10] and Media Metrix [4.11] audience reports showing the site's growth. During the evening, the Web site has added what Jennewein called "an embedded reporter" in the *Union Tribune* newspaper newsroom, to file stories that were flowing into the ink-on-paper partner before the newspaper presses rolled. Jennewein said he eventually wanted to move the entire Web site staff into the newspaper newsroom, or at least to an office adjacent to the newspaper building, to try to increase editorial cooperation between the two news operations.

The site logged a million page views on a typical day in November 2003, according to Jennewein, and the number kept climbing. The site's big circulation increases were from the big breaking stories, such as the fires that swept Southern California in the fall of 2003. And, as is the case in radio and television, Jennewein said some of those attracted to coverage of a breaking story will come back to the site as regular readers. For SignOnSanDiego, according to Jennewein, quality coverage of major local news stories has been a primary driver of audience growth.

When any major story breaks, the core newsroom generates updates from its live video crews and by working the phones. When the big fire story broke, there was no wire copy at first: All of the coverage was generated in-house. The goal was to be first with the story.

"Our goal is to be the No. 1 source of news in the community, "said Jennewein, "with a one-two punch: the newspaper in the morning and the Web site updating all day."

3. IMPORTANCE OF VIDEO INTERNET NEWS. And when news breaks, whether a preemptive story such as the 2003 Southern California fires, or a more routine news conference downtown, SignOnSanDiego's goal is simple—and posted on the newsroom wall: "Beat television, and everyone else, to the story." The Web site's "Mission and Objectives" [4.12] states it more broadly: "Routinely scoop all local media on local and national headlines."

Unlike daily newspapers in some other cities, the San Diego *Union Tribune* does not own a television station in that city. By contrast, in Los Angeles, New York and Chicago, the Tribune Company owns a daily newspaper and a television station. And in Chicago, the editorial resources of both the *Tribune* newspaper and WGN television, both owned by the Tribune Company, contribute to the Tribune-owned ChicagoLand local all-news channel (see section 2.2.5, above) and online local news services. In many other cities, local daily newspapers have partnered with local television stations and/or cable television outlets. But in San Diego, the *Union Tribune* Web site has taken a different course:

"We use City News Service [4.13] to beat television," said Jennewein, describing the site's use of a regional wire service to update text and photos on the site. But now, he said, that competition includes beating television to the story with live pictures and video packages—even though the Web site has no television partner.

"For us this is very important," said Jennewein. Analyzing the site's traffic, he and James said they found the preponderance of users—around 80%—were joining on broadband connections.

"That's why we have video news," said James. And now the site's audience expects it. Jennewein pointed to a typical day in November when the site logged 45,000 video downloads, which he compared to the audiences of San Diego television stations.

"I know this is apples and oranges," Jennewein said, but he noted the largest audience for a television newscast in San Diego had an audience rating of 5.6. In San Diego's universe of 1 million households, 5.6 % of households would be approximately 56,000. Comparing downloads to households is, indeed, "apples and oranges," but Jennewein's point was that the Web site viewed television news as its new primary competitor.

That competition is not just about numbers: It's about journalism and awards: SignOnSanDiego provided live video coverage of local news and traffic *before* local TV stations, in most cases, according to Jennewein. Video footage from the Web site also was being fed to Associated Press TV, competing with footage from San Diego television stations. And SignOnSanDiego won a local Press Club award for a television story produced by the Web site on illegal immigration. Seems there's a new television newsroom in town.

4. PRODUCING LOCAL TV NEWS ONLINE. To produce its video news, SignOnSanDiego.com has five electronic field cameras of its own, five edit stations in-house and two portable edit stations to feed produced packages live from the field. James said he opted not to use small digital video cameras,

preferring full-size ENG cameras that shoot digital video but look just like the cameras from the local television stations.

"If you get out a little, small camera," said James, "people [newsmakers] don't take you seriously." He added that everyone in the newsroom was cross-trained, so everyone could shoot and edit. According to James, the Web site was routinely first with local news stories, ranging from government news conferences to police action.

In addition to covering the news with its own ENG gear, the site also began using live video from a helicopter, which it shares with a local television station, and a number of live webcams covering downtown San Diego. Jennewein and James said the live feeds were especially important for coverage of local traffic and spot news stories before local television could get to them. The newsroom also maintained a rolling twelve-hour archive of live video that had been fed into the newsroom, so highlights packages could be easily produced. And the site was planning to use more and more live video as it developed.

"Real-time use of video is something we will experiment with," said Jennewein. To go live from more local stories, James said he wanted a full-scale satellite newsgathering truck, but Jennewein said he would have to make do with video fed by far less expensive satellite telephones—the same gear used to feed live television pictures from Iraq.

In addition to filing breaking news stories, the site's video crews were starting to produce regular programs.

"Now we are producing 'radio' programs," said Jennewein, using *Union Tribune* newspaper columnists and other experts. [4.14] During the fires, the site produced a regular program devoted to helping fire victims. Jennewein called it radio, but with a camera in the studio, it was also television. All of this was done without any television or radio news partner.

"The key question for us is, 'What does that give us that we don't already have?' " said Jennewein. "If you don't own a convergence partner, you may just be promoting the partner and not gaining anything yourself. We're completely into convergence but without a local TV station."

"We converged ourselves," added James.

San Diego may have been in the vanguard, but it was not unique: Leonard Apcar, editor in chief of *The New York Times* Internet site, predicted in 2003 that 2004 would be the year video news takes off on Web sites.

"Video as a storytelling device can no longer be ignored —especially by newspaper-oriented sites—or downplayed," said Apcar [4.15] in remarks at the 2003 annual conference of the Online News Association. [4.16]

5. COMMUNITY LEADERSHIP. Many newspapers have grown to financial leadership by embracing a mission of community leadership. SignOnSanDiego has embraced a similar mission, adjusted for the new medium. Called the City of the Future, the project drew upon experts in arts, technology, architecture and other fields, all planning for the future of San Diego. The Web site created for the project by Jennewein's staff is "Envision San Diego," [4.17] but James simply called it "Idea Central."

"You'll have a sense of leadership," he said.

The site also heavily promotes community events, Red Cross donation drives and other civic initiatives, using banner ads and other online tools. The site has a special section [4.18] where all of these outreach programs are aggregated. It's all part of what Jennewein called "increasing awareness" through community involvement: For every banner ad on the Web site, there is a real banner at the community event with SignOnSanDiego.com prominently featured.

6. EMBRACING READER-PRODUCED NEWS. Jennewein and James had been experimenting with different

editorial forms in recent years, but during the Southern California fires, they said local newsrooms were overwhelmed with information—and with requests for information. So as the story developed, the site developed new tools to report and to share information.

One was a fire blog, started by newsroom staffer Jeff Dillon, who said they already had the blogging software and were pressed by breaking events.

"The newest stuff doesn't go into the inverted pyramid," explained James. Dillon and other journalists would simply add new information to the fire blog as it was confirmed, rather than try to rewrite the story with traditional new leads. That, said James, has become part of "the new model" for covering a huge breaking story.

"The fire really showed the power of newspaper Internet sites," said James. "We had people thanking us for coverage. There was no other way to get it."

And many of those visitors to the site began to help provide information, in a reader-reported online forum.

"In the forum, people wanted pictures," James explained, "and they wanted news of specific houses." Readers wanted to know whether their houses were in danger, or how their relatives were faring. And James said readers started to connect with each other, using the Web site's interactivity.

"We built these self-help communities," he said, building on forums earlier in 2003, where relatives of American soldiers in Iraq shared pictures and formed support groups. "It's not just what we do. It's what people [readers] bring. This is the future."

In 2003, SignOnSanDiego began its first opinion blog, to incorporate views outside of the newspaper or the Web site, going well beyond the traditional op-ed page. That grew into an entire weblog section [4.19] featuring several regular contributors.

"It's a way to bring in other voices," said James, who

noted the need to delineate clearly "what's ours vs. outside contributors. Other voices can make a newspaper nervous." "But if we don't do it," he added, "someone else will."

7. CIRCULATION   GAINS,   REVENUE   AND PROFITABILITY. In November 2003, SignOnSanDiego.com passed Yahoo.com to become the most widely used Web site in San Diego, according to Jennewein, reaching more than 30% of the households in the San Diego metropolitan area. That's the second largest market penetration in the country, he claimed, second only to Washingtonpost.com.

SignOnSanDiego also drew a substantial number of readers from outside of the San Diego metropolitan area. Jennewein said their analysis of the site's traffic indicated almost half of the readers are from other parts of the U.S. and overseas. Jennewein said that realization led to the creation of a "hospitality" section of the site [4.20] and a dedicated online advertising unit, targeting hotels, car rentals, restaurants and other businesses catering to visitors. By the end of 2003, hospitality had grown to be the second largest source of online revenue, according to Jennewein, second only to real estate—another section that targets out-of-towners, those who might be moving to San Diego.

Twenty-five staff members are in advertising and support, including specialists in key advertising areas: real estate, hospitality and retail. For some, local online advertising was an extension of a long-standing relationship with the *Union Tribune*. But for many advertisers, they are new accounts and new revenue for the company.

"This is the way you get [new advertisers] into the newspaper," explained Jennewein, adding that his advertising staff builds Web sites for many of his advertisers.

Unlike many newspaper Web sites, Jennewein said, SignOnSanDiego was doing better than break-even. In 2004,

Jennewein predicted, 8% to 10% of the entire profit of the Union Tribune Publishing Company will be generated by the Web site.

And remember all of that video on the site? SignOnSanDiego.com and other sites are beginning to experiment with advertising that closely resembles television commercials. [4.21] Just as "television" news was on a newspaper Web site, "television" advertising could migrate there, too.

8. OPPORTUNITY FOR FUTURE GROWTH: TECHNOLOGY. Jennewein said most newspaper Web sites stopped research and development in 2000, essentially freezing their technology because of the dot-com collapse. Instead, said Jennewein, he went in the other direction, *increasing* research and development starting in 2000.

"We try to think about what a TV station would have done in 1955," said Jennewein.

One technology they were developing was 360-degree panoramic photography, building on research at Columbia, USC's IMSC laboratory and elsewhere, to enable visitors to select their own view of a story or to become immersed in a local event. (For more discussion of these new display technologies, see "TV News on Cell Phones," 2.4.3, above.)

Other technologies were designed to deliver local news to new devices, taking advantage of rapidly rising non-browser Internet use [4.22]. Jennewein said 1,000 people have subscribed to SMS text messaging, and by late 2003 traffic totaling 50,000–60,000 page views per month was coming from Web site visitors using BlackBerrys and other handheld devices. [4.23]

"News sent to BlackBerry will take off in another year," he predicted. "Why not develop for this sort of device?"

9. OPPORTUNITY FOR FUTURE GROWTH: SPANISH LANGUAGE. Given its location in Southern

California, next to the Mexican border, it was logical for SignOnSanDiego to explore opportunities in Spanish-language coverage and coverage of neighboring communities in Mexico. The San Diego site had a link to a smaller news site in Spanish [4.24], and it was considering cross-linking with a Mexican site, said Jennewein, providing English-language headlines for its Mexican partner and folding Spanish-language headlines into a section of the San Diego site. But Jennewein was not certain whether it made sense for his site to provide significant content in Spanish.

Jennewein did, however, say he saw opportunities for advertising to cross-border shoppers, both for Mexicans coming to San Diego stores and for U.S. residents planning a trip south of the border.

"Just look at the people shopping here," he said, pointing to the crowds at the shopping center next to the Web site's newsroom.

4.3 New definitions of local—and local news

Newspaper Web sites in San Diego and other cities are discovering that a substantial percentage of traffic comes from outside their metropolitan areas, in effect creating a larger community of San Diego, or Dallas or Cleveland. By contrast, the Web site of one Los Angeles newspaper, *La Opinion,* created a larger community by narrowing its editorial focus and by providing public service for a small but growing minority of readers.

In contrast to the San Diego *Union Tribune* site's ending most of its service at the border with Mexico—and within Southern California at the border of English and Spanish—that is exactly where *La Opinion* defined the start of its coverage area. Echoing the success of Spanish-language radio and television, which have among the highest local news audiences in cities from New York to Miami to Los Angeles, *La Opinion*'s new local news site in Spanish quickly found an audience. What may not have been planned was that an unexpected audience quickly found *La Opinion.*

LaOpinion.com began in March 2000 as the Web site of Los Angeles' largest circulation Spanish-language newspaper. By then, the Internet was crowded with newspaper sites —and with national and international news sites in Spanish.

"We started the Web site here later than most," said Mary Zerafa, *La Opinion*'s director of new media, who runs LaOpinion. com [4.25]. "The level of Internet use was appropriate," she added, among U.S. Hispanics.

1. UNDERESTIMATING LATINO INTERNET USE. Indeed, Latinos' use of the Internet was growing more rapidly than any other group in the U.S., surpassing African-Americans by the end of the century and even moving ahead of some comparable white U.S. demographic groups. To counter Anglo (and Anglo advertisers') stereotypes of low Hispanic Internet use, Zerafa pointed to 2003 surveys by Media Metrix and others showing more than 12 million Latinos were online in the U.S. [4.26]; at 33%, that's a higher percentage of use than among white Europeans in such countries as France, Spain and Italy.

"We've done quite a bit of research on [Latino Internet] users and non-users, and we've seen tremendous growth," said Zerafa. "If you look at the U.S. Hispanic market, Internet use is the same as Germany." She added that when advertisers see those numbers, "People go 'Wow!'"

Patricio Zamorano, *La Opinion*'s online editor [4.27], put it another way: "There are more Hispanics online in the U.S. than there are in the rest of the countries in the Western Hemisphere."

One reason media buyers—and other Americans—underestimate U.S. Latino use of the Internet was that, according to Zerafa, they have relied over the years on surveys done only in English.

"We do our research in Spanish and English," she explained. "Surveys in 1998, 1999 and 2000 were all done in English, so they (only) picked up Hispanics who went to English-language Web sites." Now, however, their research has detected that Latinos online have begun to diverge from those who are not.

"There is a big gap between those who read the newspaper and those who read online, and the gap is growing," said Zamorano. "Online is more educated, more comfortable with technology, more bilingual, more professional, higher-income. And that is attractive to advertisers."

But even seeing large numbers of Latinos online, Zerafa said they decided not create a "multimillion-dollar 'build it and they will come' site," preferring to build slowly in response to reader requests.

Three years after launch, the site still had a staff of only ten, including sales, marketing and technical support. They produce 100 to 150 articles each day, according to Zerafa, plus photo galleries, special sections, the entire daily contents of the ink-on-paper *La Opinion* and what she called "channels," seven sections devoted to children, home, family and similar subjects.

And readers were endorsing a specific editorial focus.

2. PUTTING COMMUNITY FIRST. "We have a very specific editorial philosophy: community first," said Zamorano. "We put the community first with a community agenda—immigration, education and health are all very important. And we are very focused on people."

Zamorano said that meant telling stories by focusing on individuals' stories and personal experiences, especially stories about people solving problems and overcoming obstacles. And those people and experiences were almost always in Southern

California, where they could be the focus of local storytelling for national readership.

"We have a very high emphasis on service journalism," added Zerafa, for a specific target audience of those who speak Spanish in a predominantly English-speaking world. That meant providing what Zerafa called "tools for different stages: people who have just arrived [in the United States] and are in their first year, those who are in year fifteen, those from Mexico, those from [El] Salvador." Zamorano said the distinctions among these groups are "huge."

"We have a lot of respect for readers," he said. "For example, we never, never say 'illegal.' We say 'undocumented.'"

Building and maintaining credibility among the different Latino communities may also require a more "pro-active" editorial stance at LaOpinion.com than at, say, the much larger *Los Angeles Times* a few blocks away. [4.28] LaOpinion.com "participates" in elections, according to Zamorano, analyzing candidates' platforms and ballot measures with its readers in mind. But LaOpinion.com also has taken more active steps, with detailed information on voter registration, "mirroring information in the newspaper." (Shortly before each election, *La Opinion* has even run voter registration forms as inserts in the newspaper.)

The Web site has sponsored regular town hall meetings across Latino communities in Southern California, meetings designed to inform the community and to inform LaOpinion. com reporters, who prepare reports based on leads from the community forums.

"We are unique," said Zamorano. "We have our feet on the street and deep roots in the community." The Web site and the newspaper have become active platforms for discussion, he added. LaOpinion.com reporters "go to the community to focus the discussion, on problems with the police, health, immigration, get people to participate at town meetings, focus on local organizations and neighborhoods. Then that can lead to a series of articles."

The emphasis on community has led to a number of awards, according to Zerafa, including *La Opinion* winning the award for best Hispanic newspaper in 2002 and again in 2003. [4.29]

(And this was not unlike the strategy at many public radio stations; see section 3.3, "Public Radio Focuses on Local Community," above.)

3. THE WHOLE WORLD IS LOCAL. Zerafa said LaOpinion.com had begun to export its "Community First" model for news coverage in other countries, starting with Mexico. A former reporter for the newspaper was holding town meetings there focusing on Mexican politics—and LaOpinion. com mirrored that coverage by holding town meetings in the U.S. about elections in Mexico—all for readers on both sides of the border.

And despite, or because of, this focus on community, LaOpinion.com began to attract an unexpected audience: readers from all over the world. When the site began in 2000, 85% of readers were from Southern California, according to Zerafa, but now she said that number has dropped to 55%–60%.

"We are filling a void," said Zerafa, "with more and more readers in New York, Texas, Florida. But Southern California is still the most important market" for Hispanics.

First, Latino readers in other parts of the U.S. discovered the site. And related or not, LaOpinion.com may more explicitly embrace a national audience: In early 2004, *La Opinion* announced it would become the hub of a new national chain of Spanish-language newspapers. [4.30]

By 2003 LaOpinion.com had begun attracting significant traffic from Argentina, Colombia and other countries in Latin

America. The site's editors quickly became more aware of the national and international audience.

"The newspaper is local, but online is universal," said Zamorano. "One permanent question for us: Should online be as local as the newspaper? If the local lead is too local, the Web site will go with Iraq or another national story." But he added that, while LaOpinion.com may use a national lead from time to time, it will not reduce its community coverage.

This focus extends to its enterprise projects, where resource limits force discipline and selection.

"We pick our targets," Zerafa explained, describing a recent example: "For the World Cup, we had the best reporting and the best history." And then there was a practical consideration: "We can reuse the World Cup section design in the future, for all championship sports."

Zerafa saw that as her Southern California Web site had become global, the competition was now CNN en Espanol [4.31], Univision [4.32] and sometimes the *Nuevo Herald* in Miami [4.33], runner-up to *La Opinion* for best Hispanic newspaper. But that did not stop her from working with a competitor:

"We did a special section for the Latin Grammys partnered with *Nuevo Herald*," said Zerafa. "We work together with other online organizations because we all only have limited resources, and egos don't get in the way."

Zerafa said the site is providing regular features requested by readers, including Mexican football (soccer) [4.34], horoscopes [4.35] and a daily newsletter e-mailed to subscribers. And for the immediate future, she said she was planning more frequent updates to the site, a more dynamic front page and new sections. She said she might even change the format for weekends, leading with different sections, citing Boston.com as a model. And she wanted to use more images and video.

"One struggle in-house is to be more visual, with photo galleries, streaming video," she explained. "We can't compete with the flood of video at CNN en Espanol, but we can co-exist."

The site's new national and international profile raises interesting questions: Why would someone in Guatemala or Bolivia head for a local Los Angeles Web site? Zerafa said readers outside of the U.S. may go to LaOpinion.com's Latin America section [4.36] for more objective news about their countries than their local broadcasters and newspapers were providing.

"There is a perspective on the news that they cannot get in their country," she explained. But she added that readers outside the U.S. wanted the same service features as readers in Los Angeles. "At our site they find out what kinds of jobs are available, how much housing costs."

"We get e-mail every day asking for jobs, complaints about human rights in their countries, complaints about justice," said Zamorano. "We try to be more progressive in our news coverage on immigration, justice and civil rights."

He and Zerafa said they had just returned from a speaking tour in El Salvador, where they had been invited to address newspaper and Internet groups about their work. And often there was a specific bottom line: For example, Salvadorans they met wanted to connect with Salvadorans in the U.S. to provide banking services to the large number of immigrants who send money home. But on this new global stage, Zerafa said they must keep the site focused on its core mission: community first.

"We cannot be all things to all people," she said. "We need to have a clear view of what we are."

PART V: CONCLUSION, AND FUTURE NOTES

I'm not bad, I'm just drawn that way.
　　　—Jessica Rabbit, in "Who Framed Roger Rabbit"
　　　(1998)

Many examples of excellent journalism in local television, radio and online news have been identified in this research, from large cities to small communities. However, just as Jessica Rabbit's notoriety came as she was characterized, so too is local news widely derided by media writers, so much so that its inferiority is a widespread assumption.

One contributing factor to negative media characterizations and to buffoonish Hollywood charicatures (think "Ron Burgundy," as opposed to, say, "Network News") is where they are conceived: The media capitals of New York and Los Angeles may not be as well served, especially in local television news, as smaller cities and towns in other parts of the country.

"Network affiliated stations tended to produce higher quality newscasts than network owned-and-operated stations ... by a large margin," notes Tom Rosensteil, director of the Project for Excellence in Journalism. [5.1]

All of the network affiliated stations in Los Angeles and New York are network-owned, so one would expect significantly lower quality local TV news in the very cities where most national media writers and critics live.

But even as many media writers deride local broadcast and online news, it was still popular with the American public. Fully four-fifths of Americans have a favorable opinion of local television news—about the same as have favorable opinions of their local newspapers, according to a 2005 Pew survey [5.2]. Those numbers were slightly higher than the comparable favorable views of network TV news—75%—and substantially higher than for national newspapers, which garnered support of only 61% of the public.

Interestingly, there was a large and growing gap between whether Americans have a favorable opinion of our local newscasts and newspapers and whether Americans believe the news they see, hear and read. The biggest gap was for newspapers—viewed favorably by 80%, but believed by only 54%, according to the Pew survey.

If local news is often underrated by media critics, the rate at which local news is changing is all but unnoticed.

Since 2003, when this project began, we have already begun to see shifts in local news, and in opportunities for local news. Some were not unexpected: Large audiences for local Spanish-language broadcast newscasts led New York 1 to launch a 24-hour Spanish-language local news service. [5.3] But other innovations were unanticipated, many driven or enabled by technology.

One newcomer: podcasting. Two years ago, it didn't exist. Now it's a phenomenon: More than 22 million adults own iPods or MP3 players, and more than 6 million adults have downloaded Internet "broadcasts" onto portable devices, according to an April 2005 report from the Pew Internet Project [5.4]. In the three months following that report, more than 6 million new iPods were shipped [5.5]. In such numbers, it is not surprising that podcasting has emerged as a new distribution path for local news, embraced by newcomers and by such veteran local news stations as WTOP [5.6].

Podcasting and many other new services are riding on a still-rising wave of high-speed broadband access and the Internet.

"[T]he Internet has become the most important source of current information for users," according to the annual Center for the Digital Future Internet survey [5.7], and a solid majority of Americans are now online.

The New York Times online is far more popular, and nationally dominant, with more than 11 million daily visitors in May 2005, than its ink-on-paper counterpart. And the *Washington Post* on paper, declining in circulation, is eclipsed by the rise of washingtonpost.com, the third most popular newspaper site in the U.S., according to Nielsen/NetRatings, with more than 7 million daily readers. And the *San Francisco Chronicle*, a minor player nationally, is the fifth largest circulation online newspaper in the U.S. [5.8]

There is no sign this growth is slowing: Adoption of high-speed Internet service in the U.S. has grown faster than adoption of such earlier consumer staples as cable television and VCRs. Some broadcast news directors are predicting their primary interaction with viewers and listeners will be online, not on air.

But over-the-air broadcasting is not static. U.S. radio stations are changing to digital transmission, promoted as "HD Radio." This allows AM stations to be as clear as FM, and FM stations are being elevated to CD-quality audio. The new technology also allows existing AM and FM radio stations to multiplex their signals—transmit two or more programs simultaneously. So WTOP could split its signal and transmit different news stories to listeners in Washington, D.C., in Maryland and in Virginia—over the air—just as Washington's NewsChannel 8 can split its cable feed to deliver micro-local news. [5.9]

Satellite radio continued its increase, with XM radio now reaching more than 4.4 million subscribers—double the number at this time in 2004. [5.10] And both satellite companies, XM and Sirius, have added ever more—and ever more controversial—local news and information services. Since 2003 both XM and Sirius have added dozens of new channels devoted to local news, sports and weather, and they are planning still more [5.9]. This is in addition to the possible addition of localized news and information to the terrestrial transmitters (see 3.6.5, above). All of this has raised the ire of local over-the-air broadcasters.

The rise of citizen journalism has been dramatic since 2003. WABC-TV in New York City is among the local newsrooms openly inviting members of the public to contribute video.

"Just send us your video or still images right here on 7online.com, or directly from your cell phone," invites the station on its Web site [5.12].

"It allows our audience to be true eyewitnesses," Kenny Plotnik, vice president and news director of WABC-TV Eyewitness News, told *The New York Times* [5.13]. Thus WABC-TV hopes to be first on a story—and with video for which the Disney Company, owner of WABC-TV, was not offering any payment. [5.14]

The ascent of citizen journalism has been even more dramatic in other parts of the world. On July 7, 2005, BBC coverage of the bombing of London's transit system relied heavily on images e-mailed from eyewitnesses at the scene. In addition to creating a Web log—now becoming a standard tool in local news—the BBC memorialized the contributions from the public on its Web site [5.15]. It doesn't take a weatherman to see which way that wind is blowing.

Elsewhere in Britain, the BBC's experiment connecting to local communities continues, with its Open Center in Hull [5.16] now relocated to a new, larger and more central location

[5.17]. The BBC does not serve other parts of Britain with local news services as elaborate as the Hull experiment, but it has launched a "Where I Live" site [5.18] that brings more local news and information, county by county, to online BBC viewers.

And the rise of citizen journalism has opened the door wide to newcomers in Asia, where broadband use is far higher than the U.S. or Europe. In Korea, OhmyNews has 33,000 registered "citizen reporters" contributing stories to a site [5.19] attracting 2 million readers a day. [5.20] Using the slogan, "Every Citizen Is a Reporter," OhmyNews has changed the Korean journalism landscape and even Korean politics. And by the way, OhmyNews is making a profit.

The success of OhmyNews has been followed by several new U.S. sites. Wikipedia's Current Events section [5.21] gave birth at the end of 2004 to Wiki News [5.22], which by June already claimed 170 citizen journalists as contributors.

The rise of citizen journalism and its impact on the journalism profession may well be the single most significant force affecting local news in the U.S. in the near future.

The proliferation of neighborhood-level local news site, such as northern Virginia's Back Fence sites [5.23], are drawing attention from the major metropolitan news sources, with implications for the economic viability of large-newsroom journalism.

Back Fence is among the sites that promote themselves as nonprofessional, proclaiming it is "written entirely by you and your neighbors. No one else knows what's happening in your neighborhood as well as you do." [5.24]

Everyone is invited to participate, not just journalists in a newsroom. And the emphasis is on micro-local news:

"What's happening with the new development down the street? Does anybody know a good house painter? Who won the T-ball championship? What's the best place in town to find good Thai food? Have you seen the photos from the church fundraiser?

Who's going to be the new junior high school principal? Anybody got tips about good bike trails? When is the next PTA meeting? These are the kinds of questions and conversations that constantly take place among neighbors—the shared wisdom of the local community. The kinds of things that used to be talked about over the back fence." [5.25]

Perhaps even more troubling to the economics of established journalism, whether on paper, on the air or online: Placing a classified ad on Back Fence is free. Craigslist.com also features free classified advertising, on a huge scale, and that already has newspaper sales departments looking over their shoulders.

Historians will look back at the early 21st century as a turning point, when decades-long patterns of reading, listening and viewing were disrupted by new, powerful and inexpensive technology.

Farley, Jennewein and Zerafa are among those who are creating opportunities, enabled by this period of technological change, to improve local news. But too many news managers are defensive or bewildered by change, just as many were bewildered in earlier centuries by carrier pigeons and the telegraph, content to watch their audiences dwindle as bloggers from the outside and newsroom missteps on the inside erode their credibility.

Meanwhile, innovators, from Korea's huge OhmyNews to the Erickson community's grass-roots channel 99, have demonstrated that citizen journalism is a major and growing factor in local news and information. Editors in long-established newsrooms may scoff at the newcomers and their lack of professional journalism experience. But by connecting to local communities more effectively than many traditional newsrooms have, the most successful newcomers may have both illustrated a weakness and highlighted a future strength of local news.

How all of this changing technology enables and propels the evolution of local news is very uncertain. All of which makes it a fruitful and interesting field of study—and for a rapidly changing and expanding array of sources of local news.

ACKNOWLEDGEMENTS

This report was conceived, inspired and guided by Geoffrey Cowan, dean of the USC Annenberg School for Communication, so it is only appropriate that he be acknowledged first. Geoff created the Local News Initiative and gave it shape, aided by a seemingly endless Rolodex with just the right contact for the next interview. His enthusiastic support for this research despite (or because of) its leading in directions quite unexpected for us both was a steady and steadying force pushing forward.

Ed Fouhy joined this project on short notice and proceeded to spend countless hours reviewing, questioning and shaping this report. A colleague and sometime boss for more than four decades (is that possible?), Ed has never wavered from certain absolutes, accuracy and clarity among them, and to the extent the pages that follow are readable and follow one to another, I am in his debt.

Many colleagues, former colleagues, friends, friends of friends and total strangers were generous with their time and insights. Some are quoted and so appear in footnotes and other sources in the appendix, but most are not; to all of those who helped, named and unnamed, I am most grateful.

Finally, an acknowledgement of history and its baggage: Biography is often a large measure of destiny, so readers will easily recognize repeated references in this report to CBS News, WINS, National Public Radio, several public television entities and now USC's Integrated Media Systems Center. These are all venues where the author has found professional homes for tenure short and long, so experiences there have certainly informed this research. Those who say former colleagues and employers have been singled out for praise or for criticism are correct.

APPENDIX: FOOTNOTES

[1.1] Michael Powell, former chairman, Federal Communications Commission, interview published in *The New York Times* magazine, September 21, 2003, page 17, and online at http://www. nytimes.com/2003/09/21/magazine/21QUESTIONS.html.

[1.2] See chart 27 and related data at http://www.rtnda.org/radio/ importance/.

[1.3] See "Reports and Surveys," Project for Excellence in Journalism, posted online at http://www.journalism.org/ resources/research/reports/default.asp.

[1.4] See "TV News Goes Back to Basics," by Jim Rutenberg, *The New York Times,* July 3, 2000, online at http://www.nytimes. com/library/financial/070300tube-wbbm.html.

[1.5] The demise of the new format was the subject of a discussion on PBS. See "WBBM Revisited," on "The NewsHour With Jim Lehrer," February 7, 2001. The transcript is posted online at http://www.pbs.org/newshour/bb/media/jan-june01/wbbm_2-7.html.

[1.6] Nigel Kay, head of journalism department, BBC Nations and Regions, interviewed at his office, 2661 Broadcasting House, London W1A 1AA, England, on January 9, 2003.

[1.7] *Arcadia,* by Tom Stoppard, Faber & Faber, 1993.

[2.1] *Television: An International History,* Anthony Smith, editor, Oxford University Press, 1995, p. 120.

[2.2] "Local TV News Project—2002: Pessimism Rules in TV Newsrooms," by Deborah Potter, Project for Excellence in Journalism, posted online at http://www.journalism.org/resources/research/reports/localTV/2002/pessimism.asp.

[2.3] "Public's News Habits Little Changed by September 11: Americans Lack Background to Follow International News," Pew Research Center for the People and the Press, June 9, 2002, online at http://people-press.org/reports/display.php3?ReportID=156.

[2.4] Deborah Potter, executive director, NewsLab, interviewed at her office, 1900 M St. NW, Suite 210, Washington, D.C. 20036, February 4, 2003. Newslab was discontinued in late 2003, but its Web site remained active at http://www.newslab.org.

[2.5] More at http://www.sbgi.net/business/news.shtml.

[2.6] See "Centralcasting on the move," *Electronic Media,* January 27, 2003, online at http://www.emonline.com/newspro/012703centralcasting.html. See excerpts and an analysis of the Sinclair experiment at "Centralcasting," "The NewsHour With Jim Lehrer," December 11, 2003, at http://www.pbs.org/newshour/bb/media/july-dec03/newscentral_12-11.html.

[2.7] "Local TV News Project—2002: How Strong is the Case for Quality?" by Atiba Pertilla and Todd Belt, Project for Excellence in Journalism, online at http://www.journalism.org/resources/research/reports/localTV/2002/quality.asp.

[2.8] Paula Madison, president and general manager, KNBC

Television and Telemundo Stations, 3000 W. Alameda Ave., Burbank, CA 91523-0002, interviewed at her office, April 3, 2003. (In 2000, Madison was promoted from head of WNBC-TV News in New York City to president/general manager of KNBC-TV Los Angeles; see http://www.nbc4.tv/ News/1330808/detail.html.)

[2.9] Will Wright, executive producer, CBS News, 524 W. 57th St., New York, NY 10019, interviewed at the Radio-Television News Directors Association convention, Las Vegas, on April 9, 2003. (In 2002, Wright returned to CBS News from WWOR-TV to produce news programming for co-owned Black Entertainment Television; see http://www.bet.com/articles/0,,c3gb-2364,00. html. He is now general manager of Voom HDNews [http:// www.voom.com/vhdo/news/index.jsp].)

[2.10] "Local TV Eye-Opener: Politics Aren't Poison," American Journalism Review, March 2003, online at http://www.ajr.org/ Article.asp?id=2798.

[2.11] "USC Annenberg Announces 2003 Winners of the Walter Cronkite Award for Excellence in Television Political Journalism," University of Southern California, March 17, 2003, online at http://ascweb.usc.edu/news.php?storyID=30.

[2.12] "Does Ownership Matter in Local Television News? A Five-Year Study of Ownership and Quality," Project for Excellence in Journalism, April 29, 2003, online at http://www.journalism.org/ resources/research/reports/ownership/default.asp.

[2.13] Non-Stop News: A Look at 24-Hour Local Cable News Channels, Local News Channel Directory, Radio-Television News Directors Foundation, 2002; also online at http://www. rtnda.org/resources/nonstopnews/directory.html.

[2.14] Available on the Web at http://www.ny1.com/.

[2.15] Available on the Web at http://www.news12.com/.

[2.16] *Cable Developments 2002*, "Regional Cable Program Services," Pages 171–194, National Cable and Telecommunications Association, 2002.

[2.17] Stephen C. Miller, assistant to the technology editor, *The New York Times*, 229 W. 43rd St., New York, N.Y. 10036, interviewed by telephone on February 20, 2003.

[2.18] Paul Sagan, president, Akamai Technologies Inc., interviewed at his office, 8 Cambridge Center, Cambridge, MA 02142, on February 24, 2003.

[2.19] Robin A. Smythe, general manager, Central Florida News, 1364 E. Concord St., Orlando, FL 32801, remarks at the Radio-Television News Directors Association convention, Las Vegas, April 9, 2003, and subsequent interview in Las Vegas later that day.

[2.20] Paul Koplin, president and chief executive officer, Venture Technologies Group LLC, interviewed at his office, 5670 Wilshire Blvd., Suite 1300, Los Angeles, CA 90036, on February 13, 2003.

[2.21] See "Univision's WXTV Ranks No. 1 in New York," MediaWeek.com, August 3, 2005, online at http://www.mediaweek.com/mw/news/tvstations/article_display.jsp?vnu_content_id=1001008886.

[2.22] See, for example, a profile of the Korean Broadcasting Network in "Ethnic Media Caters to a Big Melting Pot," *Washington Post* Fairfax Extra, April 10, 2003, page T20.

[2.23] "Reports and Surveys," Project for Excellence in Journalism, posted at http://www.journalism.org/resources/research/reports/default.asp, also cited in [1.3], above.

[2.24] See, for example, the compilation "Best Practices in Journalism: Resources," a project of Wisconsin Public Television, on line at http://www.bpjtv.org/resources/index.cfm.

[2.25] *Best Practices for Television Journalists*, Av Westin, Freedom Forum, 2000.

[2.26] "A Guide to Bias-Free Communications at WGBH," WGBH Educational Foundation, Boston, no date.

[2.27] Greg Klein, director of research, National Cable and Telecommunications Association, interviewed at his office, 1724 Massachusetts Ave. NW, Washington, DC 20036-1969, on February 21, 2003.

[2.28] Also see *Non-Stop News: A Look at 24-Hour Local Cable News Channels,* "Orange County News," Radio-Television News Directors Foundation, 2002, and online at http://www.rtnda.org/resources/nonstopnews/orangecounty.html.

[2.29] Also see *Non-Stop News: A Look at 24-Hour Local Cable News Channels,* "Bay TV," Radio-Television News Directors Foundation, 2002, also online at http://www.rtnda.org/resources/nonstopnews/baytv.html.

[2.30] These echoed the partnership that produced the highly acclaimed weekly cultural series "Omnibus," with Alistair Cooke, that began in 1952: The program was funded by the Ford Foundation. But 15 years before the founding of public television, the series was carried by CBS—and offered for sale to advertisers. Any commercial revenue was divided between CBS, to pay the cost of network time, and the Ford TV-Radio Workshop, to recoup production costs. See *As It Happened: A Memoir,* by William S. Paley, Doubleday Co., 1979, page 257. When "Omnibus" ended, the Ford Foundation spent $100 million over ten years in support of educational (now public) television, and then in 1967 the foundation funded the Public Television Laboratory, which became PBS. Source: *Due to Circumstances Beyond our Control,* by Fred W. Friendly, Random House, 1967.

[2.31] See examples in *2003 Cable and Telecommunications Industry Overview,* Chapter IX, "Cable's Commitment to Local and Regional Programming," Page 19, National Cable and Telecommunications Association, 2003, also online at http://www.ncta.com/pdf_files/Overview.pdf.

[2.32] See "BET, Say Hello to Competition," *Business Week,* January 25, 2004, page 86. Also, "New Network for African Americans," MSNBC, October 15, 2003, online at http://www.msnbc.msn.com/Default.aspx?id=3072378&p1=0.

[2.33] Online at http://www.blackpressusa.com/.

[2.34] Online at http://www.mbcnetwork.com/.

[2.35] See also "24-Hour News Channel Aimed at Black Viewers to Launch By '04," Fox News, February 11, 2003, online at http://www.foxnews.com/story/0,2933,78308,00.html.

[2.36] Online at http://www.journalism.org/resources/research/reports/localTV/default.asp.

[2.37] Marty Haag, broadcast executive in residence, Southern Methodist University, interviewed by telephone, March 19,

2003. Haag died in January 2005; see http://www.news8austin.
com/content/your_news/?SecID=278&ArID=94700.

[2.38] "Haag Joining AR&D," *Broadcasting and Cable,*
October 9, 2000, also online at http://www.broadcastingcable.
com/index.asp?layout=story_stocks&articleid=CA20041.

[2.39] "Local TV News Project—2002: After 9/11, Has Anything
Changed?" by Wally Dean and Lee Ann Brady, Project for
Excellence in Journalism, posted online at http://www.journalism.
org/resources/research/reports/localTV/2002/postsept11.asp.

[2.40] Eugene Roberts was managing editor of the *New York Times*
and executive editor of *The Philadelphia Inquirer.* He now teaches
at the University of Maryland; his biography is posted online at
http://www.journalism.umd.edu/faculty/groberts/cv.html.

[2.41] "Connecting the Community and Local News," from the
PBS Web site for its "Local News" documentary series, posted
online at http://www.pbs.org/wnet/insidelocalnews/.

[2.42] Kojo Nnamdi, host, "Evening Exchange" on WHUT-
TV and "The Kojo Nnamdi Show" on WAMU Radio,
interviewed at WAMU Radio, American University Brandywine
Building, Washington, D.C., 20016-8082, on March 18, 2003.

[2.43] See *Non-Stop News: A Look at 24-Hour Local Cable
News Channels,* "Around the Block, Around the Clock: Local
Is the Focus for Cable-Owned News Channels in Metro New
York," Radio-Television News Directors Foundation, 2002,
also online at http://www.rtnda.org/resources/nonstopnews/
aroundtheblock.html.

[2.44] Paul K. McMasters, First Amendment Ombudsman, the
Freedom Forum, interviewed at his office, 1101 Wilson Blvd.,

22nd floor, Arlington, VA 22209, on January 27, 2003. His biography is online at http://www.freedomforum.org/templates/document.asp?documentID=12814.

[2.45] Richard C. Harwood is president of the Harwood Institute for Public Innovation. His biography is posted at http://www.theharwoodgroup.com/about/#rh.

[2.46] *Tapping Civic Life: How to Report First, and Best, What's Happening in your Community* (Second Edition), by Richard C. Harwood and Jeff McCrehan, Pew Center for Civic Journalism, and online at http://www.pewcenter.org/doingcj/pubs/tcl/index.html.

[2.47] Jan Schaffer executive director, Institute for Interactive Journalism, 7100 Baltimore Ave., Suite 101, College Park, MD 20740-3637, interviewed by telephone January 28, 2003, and at the University of Florida, Gainesville, FL, February 7, 2003. Her biography is online at http://www.j-lab.org/janbio.html.

[2.48] Online at http://www.j-lab.org/.

[2.49] Online at http://www.pewcenter.org/.

[2.50] "Core Values: Local Information Programs," Walrus Research, summer 2001. An abridged version is posted on line at http://www.walrusresearch.com/reports/doc-105.htm. Beyond these data, additional information was provided by Kathy Merritt, director, Public Media Strategies, Station Resource Group, 6935 Laurel Ave., Suite 202, Takoma Park, MD 20912, interviewed in Washington, D.C., January 29, 2003.

[2.51]   John Marvel, vice president and executive editor, ESPN.com, remarks at second annual Converged Journalism

Symposium, University of Florida, Gainesville, Florida, February 7, 2003.

[2.52] See *Megamedia: How Market Forces Are Transforming News*, by Nancy Maynard, "Generation Gap: the Soft Underbelly of Change," Pages 71–84, Maynard Partners, 2000; more at http://www.nancymaynard.com/.

[2.53] Susan Clampitt, general manager and executive director, WAMU Radio, interviewed at her office in the American University Brandywine Building, Washington, D.C., 20016-8082, on April 29, 2003. Clampitt subsequently left WAMU but remains active in public radio.

[2.54]   Edward M. Fouhy, executive director and editor, Pew Center on the States and Stateline.org, at his office, 1101 30th St. NW, Suite 301, Washington, D.C., 20007, on February 4, 2003. His biography is posted at http://www. pewcenter.org/about/fouhy.html. More than a year after this interview, Fouhy agreed to serve as editor for this report.

[2.55] Bill Kovach, founding director and chairman, Committee of Concerned Journalists, interviewed at his office, 1900 M St. NW, Suite 210, Washington, D.C., 20036, on January 29, 2003. His biography is posted at http://www.journalism.org/who/ccj/ people.asp.

[2.56] Steve Paulus, senior vice president and general manager, New York 1, 75 Ninth Ave., New York, N.Y. 10011, remarks at the Radio-Television News Directors Association convention, Las Vegas, April 9, 2003, and subsequent interview later that day in Las Vegas.

[2.57] http://www.ny1.com/AboutNY1/staff_profiles.html.

[2.58] "About CLTV: Who We Are," posted at http://cltv.trb. com/about/station/.

[2.59] Kim Godwin, vice president and news director, KNBC-TV Los Angeles, 3000 W. Alameda Ave., Burbank, CA 91523-0002, interviewed at her office, May 6, 2003. Godwin later left KNBC-TV and is now assistant news director at WCBS-TV in New York. (see http://www.maynardije.org/columns/ dickprince/040816_prince/).

[2.60] Jonathan C. Knopf, news director and general manager, News 12 New Jersey, 450 Raritan Center Parkway, Edison, N.J. 08837, remarks at the Radio-Television News Directors Association convention, Las Vegas, April 9, 2003, and subsequent interview later that day in Las Vegas.

[2.61] http://www.ny1.com/Boroughs/index.html.

[2.62] http://www.baynews9.com/site/YourNeighborhood.html.

[2.63] Barbara Cochran, president, Radio-Television News Directors Association, interviewed at her office, 1600 K St. NW, Suite 700, Washington, D.C., 20006-2838, March 21, 2003.

[2.64] Online version at http://www.baynews9.com/site/weather. html.

[2.65] Online version at http://www.baynews9.com/site/espanol. cfm.

[2.66] More detail at http://www.ny1.com/OnTheAir/program_ guide.html.

[2.67] Michael Lasky, managing director, Stargazer Group, 4031 University Drive, Suite 400, Fairfax, VA 22030, interviewed at his office February 21, 2003. Lasky was formerly director of digital production for Bell Atlantic Video Services Company; see "Align and Conquer," *Wired,* February 1995, also online at http://www.wired.com/wired/archive/3.02/smith_pr.html.

[2.68] Tom Moore, station manager, Channel 99 (cable), Erickson Riverview Retirement Community [http://www.ericksonretirement.com/rwv/], 3110 Gracefield Road, Silver Spring, MD 20904, interviewed at his office April 25, 2003.

[2.69] Brent Hoffman, station manager, WOCV-TV (cable), Oak Crest Village [http://www.ericksonretirement.com/ocv/default.cfm], 8820 Walther Blvd., Parkville, MD 21234, interviewed at Tom Moore's office (see above) April 25, 2003.

[2.70] Richard Sambrook, director, BBC News, , British Broadcasting Corp. Television Center, Room 5601, Stage 6, Wood Lane, London W12 7RJ, England, interviewed at his office on January 7, 2003. His biography is posted at http://www.bbc.co.uk/pressoffice/biographies/biogs/executivecommittee/richardsambrook.shtml. Sambrook subsequently became head of the BBC World Service.

[2.71] Online at http://www.news8.net/.

[2.72] More detail at http://www.news8.net/inside.hrb.

[2.73] Nathan Roberts, anchor/reporter, News Channel 8, 1000 Wilson Blvd., Arlington, VA, interviewed in Washington, D.C., on February 21, 2003. His biography is posted at http://www.news8.net/news/talent.hrb?i=49.

[2.74] See http://www.hearstcorp.com/entertainment/property/ent_cable_newengland.html.

[2.75] Anthony Moor, new-media editor, *Democrat and Chronicle* [http://www.democratandchronicle.com/], 55 Exchange Blvd., Rochester, N.Y. 14614-2001, remarks at and subsequent interview at the University of Florida, Gainesville, Florida, February 6–7, 2003.

[2.76] Online at http://www.capitalnews9.com/.

[2.77] Paulus' remarks in this paragraph are from an e-mail interview on August 23, 2005.

[2.78] See http://www.rcn.com/corpinfo/NY/newyork.php.

[2.79] The heart of the BBC experiment is at BBCi Hull, on line at http://www.bbc.co.uk/humber/bbci_hull/how/index.shtml.

[2.80] See history at http://www.kcom.com/aboutus/ourhistory.shtml.

[2.81] http://www.kcom.com/.

[2.82] More details at http://www.pewcenter.org/batten/NHPR.html.

[2.83] http://nhpr.org/static/programs/specials/budget/index.php.

[2.84]   http://www.mynh.org/lib/html_files/sign_up/sign_up_nhpr.php.

[2.85] Posted at http://www.bet.com/community.

[2.86] Details at http://www.californiaconnected.org/.

[2.87] Val Zavala, vice president, news and public affairs,

KCET Television, 4401 Sunset Blvd., Los Angeles, CA 90027, interviewed at her office February 10, 2003.

[2.88] Edelman Annual Trust Barometer, January 13, 2004, online at http://www.edelman.com/news/index.asp?rd=1/13/2004_1.

[2.89] On line at http://www.repubblica.it/.

[2.90] Jack Driscoll, editor-in-residence, News in the Future Consortium, MIT Media Laboratory, Room E15-020F, Massachusetts Institute of Technology 20 Ames St., Cambridge, MA 02139-4307, interviewed at his office on February 24, 2003. Interviewed a second time by telephone on November 6, 2003. See extended discussion in "MIT Media Lab Offers a Simple Recipe for Publishing Homegrown News," by this author, Online Journalism Review, December 17, 2003, online at http://www.ojr.org/ojr/technology/1071702097.php.

[2.91] See http://www.metamorph.org/.

[2.92] Sandra Ball-Rokeach, Professor, Annenberg School for Communication, University of Southern California, interviewed at her office on March 6, 2003. Her biography is posted at http://ascweb.usc.edu/asc.php?pageID=26&thisFacultyID=7&sort=all.

[2.93] "CBS News e-vades censorship, lousy sound quality from Yugoslavia," by Gene Mater, Freedom Forum, October 6, 1999, posted at http://www.freedomforum.org/templates/document.asp?documentID=11393.

[2.94] See http://stringers.media.mit.edu/. Also see discussion in "MIT Media Lab Offers a Simple Recipe for Publishing Homegrown News," cited in 2.90, above.

[2.95] http://blogdex.net/.

[2.96] Cameron Marlow, Motorola Fellow and research assistant, Electronic Publishing, MIT Media Laboratory, 20 Ames St., Cambridge, MA 02139-4307, interviewed at the Media Lab on February 24, 2003.

[2.97] One interesting project at WHYY-FM was the War Letters Project. More at http://www.whyy.org/community/warletters/index.html.

[2.98] For more on the Open Center in Hull, see "BBC Project Hull," online at http://www.bbc.co.uk/humber/connecting/building/index.shtml.

[2.99] For more on the BBC Bus in Hull, see "BBC Project Hull: Connecting Locally," online at http://www.bbc.co.uk/humber/connecting/bus/index.shtml. More information on the community service motivation for both the Open Centers and Mobile Zone buses in "The BBC in the Community," BBC, 2002, online at http://www.bbc.co.uk/info/report2002/pdf/running_community.pdf.

[2.100] See more about training audiences to furnish viewer-produced video, with examples, at the BBC's "Telling Lives: Your Digital Stories" Web site, online at http://www.bbc.co.uk/tellinglives/what.shtml.

[2.101] Ulrich Neumann, director, Integrated Media Systems Center, interviewed at his office at the University of Southern California, January 24 and March 5, 2003. His biography is online at http://graphics.usc.edu/cgit/un.html. In 2005, Neumann stepped down as director of IMSC but continues as a researcher there.

[2.102] Mark Thalhimer, senior project director, Future of News Project [http://www.rtndf.org/resources/future.shtml], Radio Television News Directors Foundation, 1600 K St. NW, Suite 700, Washington, D.C., 20006-2838, interviewed at his office on March 21, 2003.

[2.103] "AOL Is Planning a Fast-Forward Answer to TiVo," by David D. Kirkpatrick, *New York Times,* March 10, 2003, Page C1.

[2.104] http://www.webopedia.com/TERM/M/Moores_Law.html.

[2.105] John Miller, news director of KTVT-TV, 10111 N. Central Expressway, Dallas, TX 75231, remarks at the Radio-Television News Directors Association convention, Las Vegas, April 9, 2003, and in a subsequent interview that day in Las Vegas.

[2.106] "Finns Phone It In," *Variety,* December 29, 2003, online at http://www.variety.com/article/VR1117897609?categoryid=1043&cs=1.

[2.107] See "Cell Phones That Surf for News," by Daniel Scuka, Online Journalism Review, February 6, 2003, online at http://www.ojr.org/ojr/technology/1044577803.php.

[2.108] See "Conference Panelists See Bright Future for Mobile Publishing," by Bruce Rutledge, Online Journalism Review, July 23, 2003, online at http://www.ojr.org/ojr/technology/1058998393.php.

[2.109] See, for example, "Hold It Right There, My Camera Is Ringing," *New York Times,* March 20, 2003.

[2.110] Images of Gates' designs also are posted at www.microsoft.com/presspass/images/features/2003/01-09SPOTWatches.jpg.

[2.111] See the Omnicamera Web site at http://www.columbia. edu/cu/record/23/20a/omnicamera.html.

[2.112] See, for example, "Gates: News on Every Wrist," by Staci D. Kramer, Online Journalism Review, January 14, 2003, online at http://www.ojr.org/ojr/kramer/1042594145.php.

[2.113] John Markoff, technology reporter, *The New York Times*, interviewed by telephone September 17, 2003. More of this interview is posted in *"New York Times* Reporter Has Seen It All Before, and He's Still Pessimistic," by the author, Online Journalism Review, October 16, 2003, online at http://www.ojr. org/ojr/technology/1066258791.php. One biography of Markoff is posted at http://www.takedown.com/bio/markoff.html.

[2.114] An American version of "Max Headroom" also was produced. See http://www.ojr.org/ojr/technology/1066258791. php.

[2.115] A reference to *Mirror Worlds, or the Day Software Puts the Universe in a Shoebox: How It Will Happen and What It Will Mean* by David Gelernter, Oxford University Press, 1991. More on Gelernter at http://www.cs.yale.edu/people/faculty/gelernter. html. And see discussion at http://sohodojo.com/ribs/mirror.html.

[2.116] Published in *The New York Times* on February 9, 2003.

[2.117] See discussion of issues raised by this technology at "Growing use of satellite images not without risks in news," by Cheryl Arvidson, Freedom Forum, March 26, 1999, posted online at http://www.freedomforum.org/templates/document. asp?documentID=11487.

[2.118] A project of the Cambridge Historical Society and the MIT Media Laboratory. Source: Erik Blankinship, Intel Fellow and research assistant, Electronic Publishing, MIT Media Laboratory, Massachusetts Institute of Technology 20 Ames St., Cambridge, MA 02139-4307, interviewed at the Media Lab on February 24, 2003.

[2.119] More at http://www.openmind.org/FAQs.html.

[2.120] Walter R. Bender, executive director and senior research scientist, MIT Media Laboratory, 20 Ames St., Room E15-208, Massachusetts Institute of Technology, Cambridge, MA 02139-4307, interviewed at his office on February 24, 2003. His biography is posted at htp://www.media.mit.edu/people/bio_walter.html.

[2.121] "Satellite images getting so good that journalists worry about government control," by Maya Dollarhide, Freedom Forum, May 8, 2000, online at http://www.freedomforum.org/templates/document.asp?documentID=12411.

[2.122] See "Spy Satellites Evolve into Private Eyes in the Sky," by Robert Lee Hotz, *Los Angeles Times,* June 13, 2000, posted on line at http://www.latimes.com/print/20000613/t000056002.html, and "God's Eyes for Sale," by Ivan Amato, *Technology Review,* March-April 1999, page 36, on line at http://www.technologyreview.com/articles/amato0399.asp.

[2.123] See "Through-Wall Imaging Systems" in FCC News Release, February 14, 2002, and images of May 12, 2003, demonstration at http://www.fcc.gov/sptf/events051203-photos.html.

[2.124] For more on that advertisement, and its implications, see "ISPs fight on both sides," part of a special report on "Software 2004," CNET, online at http://news.com.com/2009-1023-239700-4.html?legacy=cnet.

[2.125] "Offloading Your Memory," by Steven Johnson, *The New York Times,* December 14, 2003, and online at http://www.nytimes.com/2003/12/14/magazine/14OFFLOADING.html. Also, "Truly Total Recall," by Anna Kuchment, *Newsweek International,* June 30, 2003, online at http://www.msnbc.msn.com/Default.aspx?id=3068750&p1=0. Also see, for example, "What Was I Thinking? Memory Prosthesis," by Sunil Vemuri, MIT Media Laboratory, online at http://web.media.mit.edu/~vemuri/wwit/wwit-overview.html.

[2.126] See a discussion of selected technologies in "What New Technologies Could Mean for Journalism," posted at http://www.newslab.org/resources/sensingnews.htm.

[2.127] See "IMSC Presents Landmark Internet Concert Event," posted online at http://imsc.usc.edu/news/symphony.html.

[3.1] *As It Happened: A Memoir,* by William S. Paley, Doubleday & Co., 1979, page 125.

[3.2] "Americans Love Their Radio," Zogby International survey, October 6, 2003, posted at http://www.zogby.com/news/ReadNews.dbm?ID=743.

[3.3] http://www.rtnda.org/research/radusag.shtml, http://www.rtnda.org/radio/.

[3.4] Jim Farley, vice president, news and programming, WTOP Radio, 3400 Idaho Ave. NW, Washington, D.C., 20016-3000, interviewed at his office, April 18, 2003.

[3.5] Much of the information regarding KQED-FM and San Francisco radio news comes from David Hosley, former general manager of KQED-FM and of KQED-TV. Hosley is now president and general manager of KVIE Television, the PBS station in Sacramento.

[3.6] Jim Russell, general manager, Marketplace Productions, 261 S. Figueroa Ave., Suite 200, Los Angeles, CA 90012, interviewed at his office on July 29, 2003.

[3.7] See http://www.mpr.org/.

[3.8] See http://www.prairiehome.org/.

[3.9] See http://www.pri.org/.

[3.10] Online at http://www.scpr.org/.

[3.11] Paul Glickman, News Director, KPCC-FM, Southern California Public Radio, 1570 E. Colorado Blvd., Pasadena, CA 91106-2003, interviewed at his office on September 25, 2003.

[3.12] Anthea Raymond Beckler, senior news editor, KPCC-FM, Southern California Public Radio, 1570 E. Colorado Blvd., Pasadena, CA 91106-2003, interviewed at her office on September 25, 2003.

[3.13] The radio programs are cached online at http://www.tavistalks.com/. Tavis Smiley later moved from NPR to PRI and also added a nightly public television program.

[3.14] "KPCC Wins 12 L.A. Press Club Awards." KPCC news release, online at http://www.scpr.org/inside_kpcc/press_releases/2003/06/pr_030624.html. Full list of winners posted online at http://www.lapressclub.org/awards/45winners.shtml.

[3.15] Alicia B. Adams vice president, international

programming, John F. Kennedy Center for the Performing Arts, 2700 New Hampshire Ave. NW Washington, D.C., 20566-0004, interviewed at her office on January 30, 2003.

[3.16] Ruth Thompson, WAMU's senior director of marketing and communications, quoted in Current magazine, November 3, 2003, and online at http://www.current.org/radio/radio0320 wamu.shtml.

[3.17] Melinda Wittstock, bureau chief and executive director, Capitol News Connection [http://www.pri.org/cncnews/], interviewed in Washington, D.C., at the Pew Hispanic Center, 1919 M St. NW, on April 18, 2003.

[3.18] "WTOP News/Traffic Makes Ratings Music," *Washington Post*, July 22, 2003, and online at http://www.washingtonpost.com/wp-dyn/articles/A25807-2003July21.html.

[3.19] Ron Dungee, press secretary, District Office, Rep. Maxine Waters (and former editor, *Los Angeles Sentinel*), and Mike Murase, Rep. Waters' district director, 10124 Broadway, Suite One, Los Angeles, CA 90003, interviewed at their office on July 9, 2003.

[3.20] More on the early growth of wtopnews.com at "All News All the Time On the Air and Online." Freedom Forum, September 10, 1999, online at http://www.freedomforum.org/templates/document.asp?documentID=11605.

[3.21] See, for example, "The Resilience of Radio," Walrus Research, summer 2002. An abridged version is posted online at http://www.walrusresearch.com/reports/doc-110.htm.

[3.22] http://www.federalnewsradio.com/.

[3.23] http://www.bluegrasscountry.org/.

[3.24] http://www.vivalavoce.com/.

[3.25] Matt Drudge operates one of the most popular and controversial alternative Web sites, http://www.drudgereport. com/. Drudge claimed more than 2 billion visits to his site in 2003.

[3.26] "Hale's radio station rules the airwaves—even in New York," Seattle *Post Intelligencer,* November 13, 2003, and online at http://seattlepi.nwsource.com/tv/148110_radiohale13.html.

[3.27] Also online at http://www.radiokorea.com/. And see "Traffic Tips for Los Angeles Best Taken With a Pinch of Kimchi," *The New York Times*, July 30, 2003, page A11.

[3.28] "Digital Radio Takes Off," BBC News, May 8, 2003, online at http://news.bbc.co.uk/1/hi/entertainment/tv_and_radio/3010215.stm

[3.29] "XM Satellite Tops Big List of Winners," *Washington Post,* January 5, 2004, page E1, online at http://www.washingtonpost. com/wp-dyn/articles/A54841-2004Jan4.html. See also "This Is the Dawning of the Age of—XM?" *Business Week*, July 7, 2003, page 90.

[3.30] Richard Michalski, director, systems engineering, XM Satellite Radio, 1500 Eckington Place NE, Washington, D.C., 20002-2194, remarks and brief interview on May 14, 2003, at his office, during visit by the MIT Club of Washington.

[3.31] Letter to Federal Communications Commission from Jack Goodman, senior vice president and general counsel, regulatory affairs, National Association of Broadcasters, March 4, 2002, online at http://www.nab.org/Newsroom/PressRel/filings/SDARSExP3402.pdf.

[3.32] "Could Local Radio K.O. Satellite?" *Business Week*, January 12, 2004, page 13.

[3.33] XM Corporate Information, posted at http://www.xmradio.com/corporate_info/corporate_information_main.html.

[3.34] http://www.clearchannel.com/company.php.

[3.35] "Clear Channel Radio Brings Radio Listeners More Local Content," October 21, 2003, news release, posted at http://www.clearchannel.com/documents/press_releases/20031021_Rad_LocalContent.pdf.

[3.36] Statement by Edward O Fritts, president, National Association of Broadcasters, March 4, 2002, posted at http://www.nab.org/Newsroom/PressRel/statements/s0502.htm.

[3.37] "Cabinet Reaffirms Canadian Satellite Radio Ruling," *Broadcaster* magazine, September 12, 2005, online at http://www.broadcastermagazine.com/article.asp?id=47325&issue=09122005.

[4.1] *Weaving the Web: The Original Design and Ultimate Destiny of the World Wide Web by Its Inventor,* by Tim Berners-Lee, Harper San Francisco, 1999, Page 123.

[4.2] "Cable and Internet Loom Large in Fragmented Political News Universe," a joint report of the Pew Internet Project and the Research Center, January 11, 2004, posted online at http://www.pewinternet.org/reports/toc.asp?Report=110.

[4.3] "Low-income Internet users search for health information online," Pew Internet and American Life Project, December 14, 2003, news release online at http://www.pewinternet.org/releases/ release.asp?id=69. The full report, "Wired for Health," is online at http://www.pewinternet.org/reports/toc.asp?report=105

[4.4] Posted online at http://www.alexa.com/ratings.

[4.5] See "Newspapers Run 8 of Top 20 Web News Domains," *Editor and Publisher*, December 31, 2003, on line at http://www. editorandpublisher.com/editorandpublisher/headlines/article_ display.jsp?vnu_content_id=2059730.

[4.6] See more about broadcasters' Web sites in the annual survey conducted by the Radio-Television News Directors Association and Ball State University. The fall 2002 survey was summarized in "A Tangled Web," *RTNDA Communicator,* April 2003, Page 5.

[4.7] Chris Jennewein, Internet operations director, SignOnSanDiego.com, Union-Tribune Publishing Company, 2375 Northside Drive, Suite 300, San Diego, CA 92108, interviewed at his office on November 25, 2003.

[4.8] Ron James, content manager, SignOnSanDiego.com, Union-Tribune Publishing Company, 2375 Northside Drive, Suite 300, San Diego, CA 92108, interviewed at his office on November 25, 2003.

[4.9] See "Audience and Usage," at http://www.signonsandiego. com/media/demographics.html.

[4.10 Media Audit Program Reports; see http://www. themediaaudit.com/.

[4.11] See "comScore Media Metrix," at http://www.comscore. com/metrix/default.asp.

[4.12] "Mission and Objectives," goal 2a, updated September 11, 2003.

[4.13] "City News Service—San Diego News" is posted at http://www.socalnews.com/sdstories.html.

[4.14] See "SD Talk Radio," online at http://www.sdtalk.com/ sdtalkhome.asp.

[4.15] See "Video Killed the Text-News Star," *Editor and Publisher,* November 17, 2003, and online at http://www. editorandpublisher.com/eandp/search/article_display.jsp?vnu_ content_id=2030225.

[4.16] More conference coverage at http://www.journalists.org/ 2003conference/.

[4.17] "Envision San Diego" home page is at http://www. signonsandiego.com/communities/envision/index.html.

[4.18] "Communities," at http://communities.signonsandiego. com/default.aspx.

[4.19] See http://www.signonsandiego.com/news/weblogs/index. html.

[4.20] "San Diego Hotels and Visitor Information" at http:// entertainment.signonsandiego.com/section/hotels_visitors/.

[4.21] See, for example, "Denver Papers Sell Video Ads,"

Editor and Publisher, November 4, 2003, online at http://www.
editorandpublisher.com/eandp/news/article_display.jsp?vnu_
content_id=2016756.

[4.22] See "Non-Browser Internet Use on the Rise," *Editor and
Publisher,*January 2, 2004, online at http://www.editorandpublisher.
com/editorandpublisher/headlines/article_display.jsp?vnu_
content_id=2060808.

[4.23] For a complete list of PDA-type devices supported on
the site, see "Wireless," at http://www.signonsandiego.com/
wireless/index.html.

[4.24] http://www.enlacelink.com/.

[4.25] Mary Zerafa, director of new media, *La Opinion*, 411 W.
5th St., 7th floor, Los Angeles, CA 90013, interviewed at her
office on December 2, 2003.

[4.26] Summarized at "U.S. Hispanic Internet Usage," comScore
Networks, November 12, 2003, online at http://www.comscore.
com/press/release.asp?id=370. Also summarized at "Study: U.S.
Hispanic Internet Usage Rises," *Editor and Publisher,* November
19, 2003, and online at http://www.editorandpublisher.com/eandp/
news/article_display.jsp?vnu_content_id=2032100.

[4.27] Patricio Zamorano, online editor, *La Opinion*, 411 W. 5th
St., 7th floor, Los Angeles, CA 90013, interviewed at his office
on December 2, 2003.

[4.28] Additional detail at "*La Opinion* in the Community,"
posted (English-language version) at http://www.laopinion.
com/corporate/company_information/laop_in_the_community/
index.phtml?lang=en.

[4.29] See "*La Opinion* Named Outstanding Hispanic Daily," news release posted (English language version) at http://www. laopinion.com/corporate/company_information/press_releases/ index.phtml?lang=en&page=nahp_2003_tophispanicdaily.html.

[4.30] See "Lozanos, CPK Media Form Latino Newspaper Chain," *Editor and Publisher*, January 15, 2004, posted online at http://www.editorandpublisher.com/eandp/news/article_display. jsp?vnu_content_id=2070845.

[4.31] http://cnnenespanol.com/.

[4.32] http://www.univision.com/portal.jhtml.

[4.33] http://www.miami.com/mld/elnuevo/.

[4.34] http://www.laopinion.com/futbolmexicano/.

[4.35] http://www.laopinion.com/horoscopo/.

[4.36] http://www.laopinion.com/latinoamerica/.

[5.1] http://www.journalism.org/resources/research/reports/ ownership/default.asp.

[5.2] "Public More Critical of Press, But Goodwill Persists," Pew Research Center, June 26, 2005, online at http:// people-press.org/reports/display.php3?ReportID=248.

[5.3] http://www.ny1noticias.com/

[5.4] http://www.pewinternet.org/pdfs/PIP_podcasting.pdf.

[5.5] "IPod Sales Give Apple 75% Jump in Revenue," *The New York Times,* July 14, 2005, online at http://www.nytimes.com/2005/07/14/technology/14apple.html.

[5.6] See http://wtopnews.com/?sid=311915&nid=404.

[5.7] "Ten Years, Ten Trends," Center for the Digital Future, September 2004, online at http://www.digitalcenter.org/pages/current_report.asp?intGlobalId=19.

[5.8] See "21% of Newspaper Readers Transfer 'Preference' to Online," *Editor and Publisher,* June 16, 2005, online at http://www.editorandpublisher.com/eandp/search/article_display.jsp?vnu_content_id=1000963322

[5.9] See "With HD Sound, the Future Is Becoming a Lot Less Fuzzy," *Washington Post,* July 10, 2005, online at http://www.washingtonpost.com/wp-dyn/content/article/2005/07/08/AR2005070800288.html

[5.10] "XM Announces 2nd Quarter Results," July 28, 2005, online at http://www.xmradio.com/newsroom/screen/pr_2005_07_28.html.

[5.11] "Satellite Radio's New Local Content Riles Broadcasters," *Wall Street Journal,* July 25, 2005, online at http://online.wsj.com/article/0,,SB112225495906094590,00.html.

[5.12] http://abclocal.go.com/wabc/news/interact/wabc_2005_eyewitnessnewsteam.html

[5.13] "Armed With Right Cellphone, Anyone Can Be a Journalist," *The New York Times,* July 18, 2005, online at http://

www.nytimes.com/2005/07/18/technology/18cellphone.html
[5.14] See http://abclocal.go.com/wabc/news/interact/wabc_
2005_ewnteam_release.html

[5.15] http://news.bbc.co.uk/1/hi/in_pictures/4660563.stm.

[5.16] http://www.bbc.co.uk/humber/community/open_centre/
index.shtml

[5.17] http://www.bbc.co.uk/humber/connecting/building/index.
shtml

[5.18] http://www.bbc.co.uk/whereilive/

[5.19] http://ohmynews.com/

[5.20] "Is This the Future of Journalism?" Newsweek, June 18,
2004, online at http://www.msnbc.msn.com/id/5240584/site/
newsweek/.

[5.21] http://en.wikipedia.org/wiki/Current_events

[5.22] http://en.wikipedia.org/wiki/Wikinews

[5.23] http://www.backfence.com/

[5.24] http://www.backfence.com/learnMore.cfm

[5.25]http://www.backfence.com/about/index.cfm?page=/
members/aboutUs&mycomm=MC

Adam Clayton Powell III is director of the Integrated Media Systems Center, the National Science Foundation's Engineering Research Center for multimedia research, at the University of Southern California's Viterbi School of Engineering, and a senior fellow at the USC Annenberg School for Communication.

Prior to joining the USC faculty, he was general manager of WHUT-TV in Washington, D.C., the nation's first African American-owned public television station, adding several hours per week of local prime time programming. He also was the founding general manager of KMTP-TV in San Francisco, the nation's second African American-owned public television station, which he helped put on the air in 1991 featuring local news and public affairs.

Powell has served as executive producer at Quincy Jones Entertainment, where he produced Jesse Jackson's weekly television series and developed nonfiction television projects; vice president for news and information programming at National Public Radio; manager of network radio and television news for CBS News, and news director of all-news WINS in New York. He supervised the Internet and computer media technology programs at the Freedom Forum, with educational programs on five continents.